STREET SMARTS
from
PROVERBS

How to Navigate through
Conflict to Community

MITCH KRUSE
with D.J. Williams

First Edition: June 2017

All Scripture quotations, unless otherwise indicated, are taken from the THE HOLY BIBLE, NEW INTERNATIONAL VERSION, NIV, Copyright ©1972, 1978, 1984, 2011 by Biblical, Inc. Used by permission. All rights reserved worldwide.

Scripture quotations marked GW are taken from GOD'S WORD, ©1995 God's Word to the Nations. Used by permission of Baker Publishing Group.

Scripture quotations marked NASB are taken from the New American Standard Bible, Copyright © 1960, 1962, 1963, 1968, 1971, 1972, 1973, 1975, 1977, 1995, by The Lockman Foundation. Used by permission. www.Lockman.org.

LCCN: 2017936231

ISBN: 978-0692968086 (paperback)

Printed in the United States of America

STREET SMARTS

from

PROVERBS

TABLE OF CONTENTS

PART ONE: CONFLICT, THE FOOL AND WISDOM

1 The Cycle of Conflict   1

2 A Fool Defined — From Gullible to Godless   5

3 The Key To Unlocking Wisdom   11

PART TWO: TWELVE WORDS

4 Righteousness   17

5 Equity   27

6 Justice   35

7 Wise Behavior   41

8 Understanding   47

9 Wise Communication   51

10 Prudence   57

11 Discretion   61

12 Wise Counsel   67

13 Discipline   71

14 Knowledge   77

15 Learning   81

Conclusion   87

About the Authors   89

Study Guide Introduction

Conflict is all around us and often is found raging inside us. As history's wisest king, Solomon assembled the book of Proverbs to help emerging leaders, including you and me, to make wise choices. In the *Street Smarts from Proverbs* book, we examine the purpose of Proverbs, centering around twelve words—each fleshed out with four practical principles—that will transform your life when you apply them to the external or internal conflict you face.

Is there a pressing issue in your world that is causing you immense stress? Would you like to gain wisdom to apply to the conflict in your life? If so, this material is for you!

This study guide is designed to stand alongside the *Street Smarts from Proverbs* book. In it the chapters of the book are summarized in a shorter format for small-group leaders or participants to use to remind them of the key points in each chapter. We've also included lists of helpful questions to consider as you work your way through this study guide. Finally, there's a "Wisdom Challenge" discussion activity that will take you and your group to different stories in the Bible to apply each chapter's principles to a character or story outside the book of Proverbs. These study tools are designed to facilitate discussion as you study the principles found in the book of Proverbs, as well as the *Street Smarts from Proverbs* book.

Thank you for choosing to take this journey toward greater wisdom. May you be blessed as you read God's Word accompanied by the *Street Smarts from Proverbs* book and this Study Guide.

Mitch Kruse

Part One: CONFLICT, THE FOOL, AND WISDOM

Chapter 1

The Cycle of Conflict

Are you *caught* or *taught* in the cycle of conflict?

Conflict is literally defined as two objects attempting to occupy the same space at the same time (from the Latin words *con* meaning "together" and *fligere* meaning "to strike"). For example, conflict happens when two toddlers want the same toy, two teenagers make simultaneous plans to use the same car, or two coworkers apply for the same promotion.

In his attempt to lead the people of Israel three thousand years ago, King Solomon faced the inevitable conflict that he knew would come with his position. So when God offered him the opportunity to ask for anything from Him, Solomon requested wisdom (see 1 Kings 3:5-15). The wisdom of his first judicial decision rang throughout the kingdom in a story that demonstrated Solomon's cycle of wise conflict management—navigating through conflict to community. As word of his legendary wisdom spread, the world flocked to Solomon for his discernment in their conflicts.

A CYCLE OF CONFLICT ASSESSMENT

As we examine Solomon's first recorded decision, realize that *conflict* is either *positive* or *negative* (see 1 Kings 3:16-22). Are you living in positive or negative conflict? Maybe you have relied on your street smarts alone, and doing so has led to foolish choices. Maybe your success and knowledge in the marketplace has convinced others that you are bulletproof, yet inwardly you are still questioning what life is really all about. Maybe the conflict in your life has created a deafening noise that stops you from hearing the wise words found in Proverbs.

What would happen if you chose to trade your knowledge, your street smarts, and your selfish desires for the freedom found in the wisdom offered by the Creator? Today is the day for you to make a life-altering decision to follow God's wisdom instead of your own.

Let's try an experiment as we start down this road to finding wisdom and building community. Define the conflict that is at the forefront of your life. Is it positive or negative? Write down what two objects in your life are figuratively attempting to occupy the same space at the same time.

Conflict presents us with a *choice* for our next move that will be either *wise* or *foolish* (see 1 Kings 3:23-25).

As you write, examine whether the conflict in your life has been caused or perpetuated by a foolish choice. If so, complete the following sentence, and write it on the same note card: "I fostered this conflict when I made the choice to…"

If your choices regarding the conflict have been wise, then thank God for the wisdom that He is teaching you through the struggle, and write a brief note of thanks to Him here.

Choice brings *change* that reveals either *truth* or *pretense* (see 1 Kings 3:26).

As you look at the conflict scenario that you just wrote down, reflect on whether your choices regarding your conflict brought change that revealed truth or pretense in your life. Write down the result by completing the following sentence: "My choices regarding the conflict have revealed this change in the relationship with my counterpart: _____." Notice the correlation between wise choices and revealed truth as opposed to foolish choices and revealed pretense.

Change affects *community* that is either *deepened* or *lessened* (see 1 Kings 3:27-28). Solomon's wise choices led to deepened community, or relationships, on a national scale.

Follow these steps the next time you assess your reaction in a conflict situation. First pray, asking God to reveal to you the potential for deepened or lessened community within the relationship in conflict. Next, define the conflict—what two objects are attempting to occupy the same space at the same time? Third, examine whether your choices in this instance are wise or foolish. Fourth, reflect on the change that your choices bring to the relationship. Do they reveal truth or pretense? Finally, determine the effect your choice has on your community. Is it deepened or lessened?

Conflict presents a choice. Choice brings change. Change affects community. Community creates conflict.

Jesus was fully God and fully human, the perfect embodiment of the vertical (God's wisdom) intersecting with the horizontal (street smarts). Paul described Christ as "the power of God and the wisdom of God" (1 Corinthians 1:24). Jesus lived a perfect life, died at the center of a cross, and was raised again on the third day so that we could live in the center of His wisdom.

The question remains: Will you be *caught* or *taught* in the cycle of conflict?

QUESTIONS FOR REFLECTION

If you wrote about your conflict situation as suggested above, consider how your reaction to the conflict either lessened or deepened community. Talk about that with your small group or with a trusted friend.

Think of a few examples of positive conflict. How could you foster positive conflict, even initiate it, in your personal, family, or work life?

Think of a few examples of negative conflict and how you might wisely navigate through it to enhance relationships, or to improve community.

Give an example of a time when conflict has uncovered pretense in your life. Have you ever had a situation in which you've had to go to great lengths to cover up your pretense? What was the end result of that? Did you win? If not, how did it feel? If you did, how did that feel?

Consider the image of the cross as the symbol of vertical wisdom intersecting with horizontal wisdom. Does that idea help you to understand Jesus as the personification of wisdom in Proverbs? How?

WISDOM CHALLENGE

Read the story of Abraham and Isaac in Genesis 22:1-19. Consider the instances of both negative and positive conflict in that story, and discuss with your small group or with a trusted friend the ways in which Abraham's life was changed because of both the positive and the negative conflict in this situation. Then talk about ways that God allows these kinds of troubling situations in our own lives to teach us more about who He is.

Chapter 2

A Fool Defined
From Gullible to Godless

Our hearts start out like wet cement, and each one carries an impression: either our own handprints or the handprints of God. The former is foolish; the latter is wise. Which set of handprints do you have embedded on your heart? Solomon communicated: "Before his downfall a man's heart is proud, but humility comes before honor" (Proverbs 18:12).

Left unchecked, our hardness of heart will travel through five progressive stages of playing the fool. Through this chapter, we'll examine each of those stages in turn. As we do, examine your own heart to find out whose handprints are there.

A FOOL DEFINED

When it's initially poured, cement is wet and formable, but soon afterward it begins a hardening process that culminates as cured concrete. No longer malleable or moveable, the hardened chunk of concrete requires heavy equipment to roll in and pick it up before it can be moved. So also the gullible fool is still formable, but the godless fool has no hope unless they repent.

Have you ever played the fool? As people who pursue God's will and way, we want to avoid, at all costs, playing the role of the fool. A study of Proverbs gives us five stages of foolishness from the Hebrew language. Each of these stages represents a progression of increasing hardness of heart, from gullible to godless. Let's examine them:

1. THE SIMPLE FOOL

The simple fool is gullible. "A simple man believes anything, but a prudent man gives thought to his steps" (Proverbs 14:15). The Hebrew word for the simple fool is *peti.*

Give thought to your steps. Are you gullible to any foolish behavior? Open your calendar and examine your appointments for the week. Ask God to show you any gullible or naïve movements in your life. If He does, confess the pride underneath the foolishness (see Proverbs 28:13), humbly surrender it to Him (see Proverbs 11:2), and ask His Spirit to lead you to wisdom (Proverbs 9:10).

2. THE STUPID FOOL

The second stage in the progression toward a hardened heart is the *stupid fool* (*kesil*). He repeats his gullible behavior. "As a dog returns to its vomit, so a fool repeats his folly" (Proverbs 26:11).

The stupid fool is dangerous with money. Solomon revealed: "Of what use is money in the hand of a fool, since he has no desire to get wisdom?" (Proverbs 17:16).

The stupid fool trusts in his own heart. Proverbs records: "He who trusts in himself is a fool, but he who walks in wisdom is kept safe" (Proverbs 28:26).

Are you ready to make all this very real, very quickly for yourself? Ask your spouse or a close friend the following questions regarding your areas of potential stupidity:

Is folly evident in my life?

Do I repeat the same gullible behavior—like a dog returning to its vomit?

By biblical standards, are my time, talent, and treasures managed foolishly or wisely?

Am I chasing fantasies?

In my relationships, do I talk more than I listen?

If the answer to any of these questions is yes, examine your life to see whether you are trusting in yourself rather than God.

3. THE STUBBORN FOOL

The third stage is the *stubborn fool.* The word translated "stubborn" here is the same Hebrew word, *ewil,* that is translated in English as "evil."

The stubborn fool is right in his own eyes. "The way of a fool seems right to him, but a wise man listens to advice" (Proverbs 12:15).

The stubborn fool despises wisdom and discipline (see Proverbs 1:7). In his heart, he hardens his thoughts, choices, and feelings against connecting his life with God.

The stubborn fool is full of folly (see Proverbs 16:22). He repeats his stupidity at such a level that he is utterly filled with foolishness, which often displays itself in outbursts of anger. His pattern of folly in terms of anger management can be remembered as "quick to pick and stick." He is *quick* to quarrel (Proverbs 20:3). Solomon taught: "A fool shows his annoyance at once, but a prudent man overlooks an insult" (Proverbs 12:16). He will *pick* a fight: "Stone is heavy and sand a burden, but provocation by a fool is heavier than both" (Proverbs 27:3). He will *stick* the blame on someone else, rather than reconcile: "Fools mock at making amends for sin, but goodwill is found among the upright" (Proverbs 14:9).

Take Proverbs "stubborn fool" test:

Do you always have to be right?

Do you resist advice?

Do you despise wisdom and discipline?

Are you full of folly—repeating stupid behavior, including outbursts of anger?

Is your heart so hard that you show your annoyance at once, refusing to overlook an insult?

Is your quickness to quarrel evidenced in your provocation of more negative conflict?

Do you scoff at the thought of making amends?

If the answer to any of these questions is yes, then it is time for a heart change.

4. THE SCORNING FOOL

The fourth stage is the *scorning fool* (*letz*, in Hebrew). "The proud and arrogant man—'Mocker' is his name; he behaves with overweening pride" (Proverbs 21:24). He has moved from being teachable and having low-level but redeemable foolishness, past stubborn pride, and on to mocking.

The scorning fool is averse to wisdom. "The mocker seeks wisdom and finds none, but knowledge comes easily to the discerning" (Proverbs 14:6).

The scorning fool causes dissension in organizations. "Drive out the mocker, and out goes strife; quarrels and insults are ended" (Proverbs 22:10).

The scorning fool is opposed by God: "He mocks proud mockers but gives grace to the humble" (Proverbs 3:34).

Consider the following questions as you think about the stubborn fool:

Is it a challenge for you to separate wise choices from foolish ones?

Would anyone at work, home, or play say that you are the cause of organizational dissension?

Do you feel like you are "kick[ing] against the goads" (Acts 26:14) with God?

If your answer is yes to any of these questions, you are behaving like a scorner, and it's time for a change.

5. THE GODLESS FOOL

The fifth stage is the *secular*, or *godless*, *fool. The secular fool exalts himself rather than God.* "If you have played the fool and exalted yourself, or if you have planned evil, clap your hand over your mouth" (Proverbs 30:32).

Carefully consider your own heart.

Is there any area inside of you in which you have exalted yourself above God?

Is there any area in which you refuse to seek God's heart by way of any thought, choice, feeling, or prayer?

Are you living your life on autopilot apart from God?

Do you need more and more of your "fix" of choice to advance your own earthly kingdom at the expense of Christ's because you perceive your desires are not truly satisfied in Him?

If your answer to these questions is yes, you may be coming dangerously close to playing the secular fool.

It's easy to read through these lists describing the progressive hardening of the heart and think of someone else who fits each stage. However, the list is for our own self-examination. Each of us must ask, "Is there any area of my life where I have hardened my heart to the Spirit of God?" If we consider our answer prayerfully and ask for God's guidance, the answer will be yes more often than we think. After identifying the foolish behavior, we must confess our pride to God, humbly surrender it to Him, and ask His Spirit to lead us to wisdom.

QUESTIONS FOR REFLECTION

Review the questions embedded in the discussion above and consider whether these descriptions characterize you or someone you know. What actions can you take today to change your heart or the heart of your friend or loved one?

What do you think—can people be different kinds of fools at different points in their lives?

Can even wise people be foolish when it comes to certain choices in their lives? Can you think of an example of this?

What part do you think sanctification plays in the Christian's learning process of moving from being foolish to pursuing wisdom?

What do you think it means to you personally to have "God's handprints embedded on your heart?"

WISDOM CHALLENGE

Read the entire story of David, Nabal and Abigail in 1 Samuel 25:1-42. Consider the ways that David played the fool and how his heart was changed by the wisdom that came from Abigail. Also look again at the example of Nabal and think about a situation in your life when you either encountered a person like Nabal, or were hard-headed enough to qualify as a Nabal. What did you learn from this situation? Did a part of you have to die—maybe your pride or a cherished belief or position—in order for you to make a change?

Chapter 3

The Key To Unlocking Wisdom

THE FOUR CHAMBERS OF THE HEART: W.I.S.E.

Will

The *will* is the chamber of our *choices*. Nearly every action is preceded by a choice. In order to experience wisdom in our lives, we must surrender our will—that is, our choices—to God. Humbling our will to God in order to experience wisdom is a clear choice (see Proverbs 8:10). In essence, it is the flip of a switch.

Intellect

The *intellect* is the chamber of our *thoughts*, including all the information, images, and ideas in both our conscious and subconscious mind. The humbled intellect is open to the wisdom of God--the divine light that illuminates our hearts. King Solomon preached: "The fear of the LORD teaches a man wisdom, and humility comes before honor" (Proverbs 15:33). When we humble our intellects to God, we have the mind of Christ (see 1 Corinthians 2:16). This moves us from pretense to authenticity.

Below is a priceless approach to studying the wisdom of Christ:

- **Study Wisdom 101:** Read one chapter in Proverbs each day that corresponds with the date of the month. Proverbs has thirty-one chapters, so you will read through the book once each month during the course of the year. For months that have thirty days or less, you can either read the remaining chapters or begin anew with Proverbs 1 at the beginning of the following month.

- **Study Wisdom 201:** Follow Study Wisdom 101, plus read a chapter from the New Testament each day. This allows you to read the entire New Testament in less than a calendar year.

- **Study Wisdom 301:** Follow Study Wisdom 201, plus read three chapters each day in the Old Testament, so that you read through the entire Bible in a year.

- **Study Wisdom 401:** Follow Study Wisdom 301, plus memorize one verse each week that you apply to your daily life.

Which one will you commit to today?

Spirit

The *spirit* is the chamber of our *prayers*. The Bible refers to the spirit as the lamp of God (see Proverbs 20:27).

The acronym PRAYS is from the Lord's Prayer, where Jesus taught His disciples how to pray (Matthew 6:9-15). This five-fold pattern will transform your prayer life.

Jesus said, "This, then, is how you should pray" (Matthew 6:9):

Praise. Jesus prayed: "Our Father in heaven, hallowed be your name" (Matthew 6:9). When you pray, praise your heavenly Father for who He is (holy) and for being as close as the air around you.

Renew. Jesus prayed: "Your kingdom come, your will be done on earth as it is in heaven" (Matthew 6:10). When you pray, He will renew your mind to be about His kingdom.

Ask. Jesus prayed: "Give us today our daily bread" (Matthew 6:11). When you pray, ask God for what you need to advance His kingdom, whether it be knowledge, new ideas, relationships, clarity, or guidance.

Yield. Jesus prayed: "Forgive us our debts, as we also have forgiven our debtors" (Matthew 6:12). When you pray, yield all of your unsettled relational accounts to God.

Surrender—to be Spirit-led. Jesus prayed: "And lead us not into temptation, but deliver us from the evil one" (Matthew 6:13). When you pray, surrender your heart to be Spirit-led in order to become a rapid Holy Spirit responder.

Become a person who PRAYS. Ask God to lead you to the intersection of His heart with street smarts. Pray this request to God before, during, and after your Scripture reading as well as when you are making a significant decision or encountering another person during a divine appointment. You'll become a rapid Holy Spirit responder when you begin to pray this way.

Emotions

Our *emotions* represent the chamber of our *feelings*. These are the multiple reflectors, or mirrors, of the light in us.

Solomon not only challenged young leaders to choose wisdom (see Proverbs 8:10), but he also went on to say that they should desire it above all else: "For wisdom is more precious than rubies, and nothing you desire can compare with her" (Proverbs 8:11).

Humble your emotions to God and desire wisdom. In every encounter, desire wisdom. Feel it. Want it. Joyfully embrace it. Just as changing your diet from junk food to healthy food will create a desire for different tastes, so desiring wisdom will lead to a different appetite for life.

Remember that pride is the lock on the human heart that keeps us from pursuing the wisdom of God. Humility is the key that unlocks the gate to wisdom, and that wisdom is a person: the person of God in Jesus Christ.

When we humble all four chambers of our hearts to God, we receive Christ, who is the wisdom of God as He dwells in us through His Holy Spirit (1 Corinthians 1:24). Jesus Christ is the intersection of the vertical with the horizontal. He is fully God and fully man. He is God's heart combined with street smarts. He has reconciled mankind with God and people with one another. Paul referred to Christ in us as "the hope of glory" (Colossians 1:27). When we humbly surrender all four chambers of our hearts to God, we can be confident and assured that God's wisdom in Christ will be manifested in and through us.

QUESTIONS FOR REFLECTION

Think of three ways that you can make God's wisdom "sticky" to your life and your circumstances. (One example would be to print or write out some personally applicable proverbs and tape them to your bathroom mirror or to your computer screen.)

What does it mean for you to humble your heart to God? How do you think one could practically do this? What first steps do you take in doing so?

Which of the four chambers of the heart is the most difficult for you to humble to God's will? Which is the easiest for you to humble to God's will?

Consider one of the four chambers of the heart. How would your life change, in either small or large ways, by your humbling your heart to him in this area?

What does it mean to have a heart of clay in regard to submitting to God in these different areas of your life? Think about one specific instance in which you learned to submit to God—either the hard way, or the easy way.

WISDOM CHALLENGE

Read the entire story of David and Bathsheba in 2 Samuel 11:1—12:25. Consider the ways that David hardened his heart in the first part of the story, how he refused to surrender each of the four chambers of his heart to God. Consider the same for Bathsheba. Then consider the positive conflict that Nathan introduced to David and think about how his example of humbling himself can teach you about doing the same thing in your own life. Can you think of one specific example where this has already happened? Are you willing to consider another situation in which this might need to happen in your life? Or perhaps you can become someone's Nathan. Is the spirit prompting you as you read this story? Pray about and consider what God may be leading you to in this situation.

Part Two: TWELVE WORDS

Proverbs is the Old Testament's book of wisdom. In its introduction, Solomon reveals twelve words to the wise—twelve pearls of wisdom—that serve as the foundational teachings of this literary gem. Pursue these in order to discover a life filled with wisdom!

Learning and applying these twelve words: righteousness, equity, justice, wise behavior, understanding, wise communication, prudence, discretion, wise counsel, discipline, knowledge, and learning will significantly transform your life, allowing you to navigate through conflict to community.

Chapter 4

Righteousness

When it comes to conflict, we all want to make the right decisions, say the right words, garner the right power, and do the right thing so that we can get the right result. The only problem is that since the first sin, people throughout history have determined for themselves what is right and wrong—including us. Our perspective of right and wrong is clouded, as if we're peering through a foggy window. Consequently, we need to seek God's wisdom in order to discover His crystal-clear perspective on what is truly right.

Righteousness, *tsedeq* in Hebrew, is translated in The New International Version as "doing what is right" (Proverbs 1:3) in God's sight. It comes from God rather than the good works of any individual (see Proverbs 2:6-9). Righteousness is often juxtaposed in Proverbs with wickedness—doing what is wrong in God's sight. Left to our own pride and foolishness, we will too often choose what God calls sin over what He sees as right action.

Solomon clarified God's perspective on this: "To do what is right and just is more acceptable to the LORD than sacrifice" (Proverbs 21:3). The uses of righteousness in Proverbs uncover four contextual patterns: *righteous decisions*, *righteous talk*, *righteous strength*, and *righteous walk*.

RIGHTEOUS DECISIONS

Our major decisions surface in many area, but we're going to look at just three: career, community, and challenges. Proverbs equips us for righteous *decisions* in all three areas. Solomon penned: "The plans of the righteous are just, but the advice of the wicked is deceitful" (Proverbs 12:5). Wisdom offers us a righteous grid to process our decisions before we make them. Solomon observed: "The heart of the righteous weighs its answers, but the mouth of the wicked gushes evil" (Proverbs 15:28).

Career

Righteous decisions enrich our careers, and more frequently *in the midst of* our work than in our choice of the right profession. Though the latter carries long-term consequences, Proverbs does not neglect the weight of the former: "The wicked man earns deceptive wages, but he who sows righteousness reaps a sure reward" (Proverbs 11:18). Life flows inside out from the heart (see Proverbs 4:23). Who we are to *be* determines what we are to *do*, which determines where we are to *go*. Too often we get it backward. We believe that if we go somewhere, we will do something in order to be somebody. Consequently, it is important for us to work wholeheartedly, right where we are, sowing righteousness in order to reap a sure reward. When thinking about a career, we must remember that God cares much more about *who we are* than *what we do*.

The righteous are delivered from evil desires that stem from an unfaithful heart—one that is duplicitous and divides its loyalty. Frequently this is fleshed out as the employee leverages his or her present employer against a potential future one (see Proverbs 11:6). Solomon warned of the consequences of this alluring sin versus the reward of doing what is right in God's sight: "Misfortune pursues the sinner, but prosperity is the reward of the righteous" (Proverbs 13:21). Proverbs alludes to the fact that those who are righteous generally have employment while those who are wicked often go hungry (see Proverbs 13:25). It's generally true, most of the time, that righteous decisions regarding how we function in our careers lead to a financial cushion, whereas the income of the wicked is spelled *t-r-o-u-b-l-e* (see Proverbs 15:6).

Are you struggling with the validity of your career? Are you earning deceptive wages by not fully applying yourself? Do you think that your identity consists of what you do, and you don't like what you do? Are you searching for another job on your employer's dime, disseminating your résumé on the computer they have provided? Maybe it's time to refocus and work wholeheartedly, right where you are.

Community

Righteous decisions enhance relationships in *community* with others; wicked ones hurt them. Similarly, righteous decisions improve our relationship with God, whereas wicked decisions damage our relationship with Him. Solomon wrote: "The LORD's curse is on the house of the wicked, but he blesses the home of the righteous" (Proverbs 3:33), and "When the righteous prosper, the city rejoices; when the wicked perish, there are shouts of joy" (Proverbs 11:10). Conversely, the people groan when the wicked rule, knowing that community will be diminished (see Proverbs 29:2).

Challenges

Righteous decisions *guide* us through life's challenges. Wicked decisions *hide* us. Typically, we follow our wicked decisions with pretense in an effort to hide the source of those decisions—an unrighteous or unfaithful heart. Solomon described the guiding versus the hiding when he wrote: "The righteous man is rescued from trouble, and it comes on the wicked instead" (Proverbs 11:8); that is, the wicked get punished, but the righteous go free (see Proverbs 11:21). When referencing the challenges of life, Solomon equated the benefit of righteous decisions to freedom, and the consequences of wicked ones to a trap (see Proverbs 12:13). How many of us haven't felt the truth of that comparison in our own lives?

What decisions are you facing that require righteousness? Are you in the midst of making decisions in your career, in your community, or in your other challenges? Has your pattern been paraphrased as, "If I just *go* somewhere, then I will *do* something in order to *be* somebody"? Let who you are designed to *be* determine what you are to *do* and where you are to *go*. Read through the book of Proverbs and seek out God's wisdom and His righteousness before you make your next major decision.

RIGHTEOUS TALK

Solomon said: "The tongue of the righteous is choice silver, but the heart of the wicked is of little value" (Proverbs 10:20). Righteous *talk* is paramount if we want to live out God's wisdom for the conflict in our lives. Proverbs offers three wise traits for righteousness in our speech: honest, hopeful, and helpful.

Honest

Righteous talk is *honest*: "The mouth of the righteous is a fountain of life, but violence overwhelms the mouth of the wicked" (Proverbs 10:11). A fountain of the type that Solomon describes is pure, clear, consistent, and life-giving. Contrastingly, the words of the wicked are dishonest. They are impure, confusing, unpredictable, and life-taking. Not for nothing has the adage "Honesty is the best policy" been passed down from generation to generation. It's absolutely true.

Hopeful

Righteous talk is *hopeful*. Amid life's storms, the righteous are hopeful with their words, but the wicked are full of despair. Solomon described the aftereffects of a stormy conflict; the kind where our words can often get us into trouble: "When the storm has swept by, the wicked are gone, but the righteous stand firm forever" (Proverbs 10:25). After their heated exchanges, the wicked often flee the scene. Solomon went on to describe this hopelessness of the wicked: "The prospect of the righteous is joy, but the hopes of the wicked come to nothing" (Proverbs 10:28). Positivity characterizes a person whose hope is in the Lord, from one who trusts in God's wisdom and guidance. One who understands the free gift of God's grace and has accepted it cannot help but utter hopeful speech. Conversely, hope will not come from wicked words.

Helpful

Righteous talk is *helpful*. First, because righteous words are nourishing: "The lips of the righteous nourish many, but fools die for lack of judgment" (Proverbs 10:21). Second, they are helpful because they are wise: "The mouth of the righteous brings forth wisdom, but a perverse tongue will be cut out" (Proverbs 10:31). Third, they are helpful because they are fitting: "The lips of the righteous know what is fitting, but the mouth of the wicked only what is perverse" (Proverbs 10:32). *Fitting* is translated from the Hebrew word *ratson*, translated as "acceptable," which means "bringing favor, or good will." When our talk is righteous and helpful, we bring favor and good will to our conversations.

Each of these three traits of righteous speech is a characteristic of Christ. He is honest; namely, He is the truth of God (see John 14:6). He is hopeful; specifically, He is the hope of God for all who will believe (see 1 Timothy 1:1). He is helpful; certainly, He is the help of God for those who put their trust in Him (see Hebrews 13:6). In order for our talk to be honest, hopeful, and helpful, we must surrender our hearts to Christ. Then His wisdom and righteousness will flow through our words.

What part of your speech needs to change in order for your words to be righteous? Is your talk honest, hopeful, and helpful? Ask a close friend the answer to these questions, and begin a step-by-step process of planning to exchange your wicked words that tear down others for righteous ones that build them up. Step one is realizing that your words have either a positive or negative effect; step two is making a mental note of checking yourself when you're in conflict to understand what your approach is and how it impacts your community; step three is surrendering your inner conflict to God, and asking Him to help you to change for the better and build relationships with your words rather than tearing them down.

RIGHTEOUS STRENGTH

Often in life we try to get ahead more quickly by taking shortcuts that twist something that's wrong to make it appear right. Solomon warned of the consequences of such foolishness when he said: "A man cannot be established through wickedness, but the righteous cannot be uprooted" (Proverbs 12:3). True, enduring *strength* and success is found in the pursuit of righteousness, which provides both a foundation and framework that will endure: "Wicked men are overthrown and are no more, but the house of the righteous stands firm" (Proverbs 12:7).

This righteousness is not a righteousness that comes from our own abilities, or even our own desire to do good; rather, it is a righteousness that comes from God. Solomon wrote that nothing is stronger than the righteous identity of God: "The name of the LORD is a strong tower; the righteous run to it and are safe" (Proverbs 18:10). This righteousness is available to those who humble themselves and turn to the Lord when faced with a difficult situation. Righteousness strengthens us with: resilience, relationship, and resolve.

Resilience

Righteousness strengthens us with resilience—the ability to endure, or withstand conflict: "For though a righteous man falls seven times, he rises again, but the wicked are brought down by calamity" (Proverbs 24:16). The righteous, who look to God for direction and pursue His will for their lives, tend to experience more success and longevity in their endeavors, whereas the wicked are more likely to encounter failure: "The righteous will never be uprooted, but the wicked will not remain in the land" (Proverbs 10:30). Paul challenged believers to resilience when he said, "And as for you, brothers, never tire of doing what is right" (2 Thessalonians 3:13). *Never.*

Relationship

Righteousness strengthens our relationship with God. Solomon observed: "He whose walk is upright fears the LORD, but he whose ways are devious despises him" (Proverbs 14:2). Our bond with the divine is enhanced through prayer—the connection of our hearts with His: "The LORD is far from the wicked but he hears the prayer of the righteous" (Proverbs 15:29).

Resolve

Righteousness strengthens us with *resolve*—the motivation to manage, work out, or settle conflict. "Righteousness exalts a nation, but sin is a disgrace to any people" (Proverbs 14:34). A nation is exalted when righteous resolve flows from righteous leaders. This kind of resolve provides courage to properly manage and resolve conflict because the righteous have nothing to hide. King Hezekiah's men (see Proverbs 25:1) copied Solomon's wise saying regarding this matter: "The wicked man flees though no one pursues, but the righteous are as bold as a lion" (Proverbs 28:1).

What weaknesses of yours can be transformed into strengths through your renewed pursuit of righteousness? Would you like to experience more resilience and greater strength in the face of conflict? Are you willing to pray in order to strengthen your relationship with God? Are you in need of resolve to work out your conflict? Schedule five minutes each day on your calendar to pray that the Spirit will lead you into righteousness. Ask God directly for personal strength that is evidenced in resilience, relationship, and resolve.

RIGHTEOUS WALK

The Bible's authors use the term *walk* as a metaphor for life. The path where our feet take us comprises our life. Every single day, in a thousand different ways, we choose either a pathway toward righteousness or one that takes us toward wickedness. God's desire for us is to follow the wise pathway of righteousness. Characterizing wisdom's connection with righteousness, Solomon wrote: "Thus you will walk in the ways of good men and keep to the paths of the righteous" (Proverbs 2:20; cf. 8:20). The righteous path is free of blame; it is one that, through personal example, can be passed on to further generations: "The righteous man leads a blameless life; blessed are his children after him" (Proverbs 20:7). Jesus summed it up this way: "Wisdom is proved right by her actions" (Matthew 11:19)—heart-guarded, abundant, and eternal.

Heart-Guarded

A righteous walk is heart-guarded. Solomon wrote one of the most foundational bits of wisdom for us as humans when he penned: "Above all else, guard your heart, for it is the wellspring of life" (Proverbs 4:23). Paul said that when we fully surrender our hearts to Christ, we receive not only His righteousness, but also His prayer-inspired peace that guards our hearts like a military fortress (see Philippians 3:9; 4:6-7). Solomon described this same kind of divine protection when he wrote: "Righteousness guards the man of integrity, but wickedness overthrows the sinner" (Proverbs 13:6). *Integrity* indicates a state of being whole, of being undivided. The person who pursues integrity in all his dealings works out of a context of complete surrender to the Lord, accomplished by praying for it daily.

Abundant

A righteous walk is abundant. Solomon observed: "The light of the righteous shines brightly, but the lamp of the wicked is snuffed out" (Proverbs 13:9). A light that shines brightly illuminates abundantly, providing all of the light that we will ever need. Jesus' wisdom is that light—a light so strong and persistent we will never need another. Solomon proclaimed: "The path of the righteous is like the first gleam of dawn, shining ever brighter till the full light of day" (Proverbs 4:18). Solomon wrote: "Better a little with righteousness than much gain with injustice" (Proverbs 16:8). He concluded that a righteous walk satisfies with the hallmarks of an abundant life: "He who pursues righteousness and love finds life, prosperity and honor" (Proverbs 21:21).

Eternal

A righteous walk is eternal. According to Solomon, this kind of a walk brings life that never ends: "In the way of righteousness there is life; along that path is immortality" (Proverbs 12:28). Eternity includes judgment, one that each of us will face with God. When we do, no amount of earthly success, either in money gained or good works done, will pay for our unrighteousness. Only the righteousness of another can pay for our sin. Solomon reflected: "Wealth is worthless in the day of wrath, but righteousness delivers from death" (Proverbs 11:4). If we reject the righteousness of Christ, we will experience death—eternal separation from God. Solomon summarized: "The truly righteous man attains life, but he who pursues evil goes to his death" (Proverbs 11:19). "When calamity comes, the wicked are brought down, but even in death the righteous have a refuge" (Proverbs 14:32). Jesus Christ is indeed the refuge of those who accept His righteousness as their own and live in the pursuit of His wisdom.

What part of your *walk* needs to change in order to pursue righteousness? Where do your feet take you? That's your life. Do your steps lead you to a click, a smoke, a toke, a binge, a pop, a fix, a fling, or even a self-righteous act? Those acts that come from a selfish heart lead to your death. Are you willing to walk toward the heart-guarded, abundant, eternally righteous refuge of Christ? Your life led to His death; His death leads to your eternal life.

Jesus called us to seek first God's kingdom and His righteousness (see Matthew 6:33). No one can meet that standard by their own efforts. The only righteousness that surpasses that of the Pharisees and the teachers of the law is the righteousness of Christ Himself because He alone is the Righteous One (see 1 John 2:1). We must humble our spiritual hearts to Him in order to receive His righteousness. Then He brings His wisdom, His righteousness, into our *decisions*, our *talk*, our *strength*, and our *walk*.

QUESTIONS FOR REFLECTION

What decisions are you facing that require righteousness? Are you in the midst of making decisions in your career, in your community, or in your other challenges? How can you apply the principle of righteousness to those decisions?

What part of your speech needs to change in order for your words to be righteous? Is your talk honest, hopeful, and helpful? Ask a close friend the answer to these questions, and consider the suggested step-by-step process of planning to exchange your wicked words that tear down others for righteous ones that build them up.

What weaknesses of yours can be transformed into strengths through your renewed pursuit of righteousness? Would you like to experience more resilience and greater strength in the face of conflict? Are you willing to pray in order to strengthen your relationship with God? Are you in need of resolve to work out your conflict?

What part of your *walk* needs to change in order to pursue righteousness? Are you willing to walk toward the heart-guarded, abundant, eternally righteous refuge of Christ?

Consider how you can make changes in your life today—in your decisions, in your talk, in your strength, and in your walk—that could make a significant difference in your relationship with God and in your relationships with others. Write them down and put them in a place where you know you'll see what you've written.

WISDOM CHALLENGE

Read the story of Paul's conversion as he details it in Acts 22:1-21. Consider what Paul's life was like before Jesus confronted him and how he persecuted the church; then discuss how Paul's decisions, his walk, his talk, and where he found his strength changed after his conversion. As you do, think about your own story, and discuss how your own life has changed since you accepted Jesus as your Lord and Savior.

Chapter 5

Equity

What is fair? We often ask this question in dating, marriage, parenting, education, sports, friendships, business partnerships, ministry collaborations, and national alliances. The wisdom literature in Proverbs offers us the answer in a key word embedded in the twelve signs of wisdom. That word is equity (meyshar in Hebrew. The New International Version translates equity as "doing what is...fair" (Proverbs 1:3). In a world where some say, "God isn't fair," the Bible speaks to the contrary: "God is fair" (Hebrews 6:10; cf. Psalm 145:17 GW).

Proverbs provides insight into how we apply not only *what* is fair, but also *who* is fair to those occurrences in our lives when we experience conflict. A study of Solomon's uses of the Hebrew word for *equity* in his book of wisdom reveals four contextual patterns to help us wisely navigate through conflict toward community. "What is fair" includes: *straight paths*, *blameless motives*, *intimacy with God*, and *integrity*.

STRAIGHT PATHS

First, we see that what is fair includes *straight paths*. Solomon passed along his father's advice, saying: "I guide you in the way of wisdom and lead you along straight paths" (Proverbs 4:11). *Straight* is interpreted from the same root as *equity*, or what is fair. That root can be interpreted as "smooth" or "evenly applied," a reference to the fashioning of metal. Paths represent our track or course of life. Typically, when we experience interpersonal conflict in our lives, we do not evenly apply the principles of risk and return between the other person involved and ourselves.

Risk is the potential for loss. *Return* is the profit, gain, or reward. When relational tension arises, we tend to pile up risk on the other party while we attempt to retain all the return. Consequently, our paths become crooked, or uneven. Wisdom's tool for evening our paths is equity that begins by placing all of the risk in the exchange on God. Solomon encouraged: "Trust in the LORD with all your heart and lean not on your own understanding; in all your ways acknowledge him, and he will make your paths straight" (Proverbs 3:5-6). When we surrender to God, we place all the risk on him for our heart's choices, thoughts, prayers, and feelings. When we trust in Him for all our ways—our time, talent, and treasures—God responds by making our paths straight, or fair. The antithesis of equity is trusting in our own imperfect understanding. This minimizes our vulnerability in an attempt to maximize our self-centered return.

Let's take a look at a well-known example of this principle. After David's sin with Bathsheba and his subsequent plot to kill her husband Uriah, the prophet Nathan explained to the king through a parable that he had been unfair (see 2 Samuel 12:1-9). The reason for the inequity was that David had taken all the return while Uriah had unknowingly assumed all of the risk. The same risk-to-return relationship is also evidenced in the balance of responsibility (risk) with authority (return). In this situation, David's responsibility was not commensurate with his authority.

In his incarnation, life, and death, Jesus offered a dramatically different example of this principle that provides insight into the heart of God. When He was treated unfairly, the One with ultimate authority equally exercised His responsibility and risked everything with His Father, trusting in God to judge what is fair (see 1 Peter 2:23). By sending to earth His Son Jesus Christ, God took all the risk to provide those who will believe in Him for salvation with all of the return (see 1 Peter 2:24).

Are your paths uneven? When relational conflict occurs, do you risk little in an effort to return much? Do you create your own limited scale of what is fair? If so, you are leaning on your own understanding rather than trusting in God. Trust in the Lord with all your hear and let Him shoulder the risk. With all your time, talent, and treasure, seek the One who is fair. He will straighten your paths by bringing equity to your conflict.

BLAMELESS MOTIVES

Solomon wrote: "The righteousness of the blameless makes a straight way for them, but the wicked are brought down by their own wickedness" (Proverbs 11:5). *Blameless* refers to our motives, which can be defined as our desires, intentions, drives, or purposes. These represent the spiritual heartbeat that connects the heart with the three resources of life: time, talent and treasure. God's perspective of equity includes peering into our hearts and weighing our motives (see Proverbs 21:2).

Blameless motives make us concerned for the things that God characterizes as fair. When our motives are selfless and in line with God's concerns, then they can be characterized as blameless. But too often in interpersonal conflict, we are selfish.

The apostle Paul wrote: "Do nothing out of selfish ambition or vain conceit, but in humility consider others better than yourselves. Each of you should look not only to your own interests, but also to the interests of others" (Philippians 2:3-4). When we find ourselves in the midst of conflict, we need to look to our own *selfless* interests, but not our own selfish ones. This is how we know that our motives are true and blameless.

As we have seen previously, doing what is fair begins with risking our heart and resources for God's glory. Our motives, or our desires, link our hearts with our resources. Paul said that *blameless motives* are a by-product of our hearts being united with Christ and having fellowship with the Holy Spirit (see Philippians 2:1).

What is fair includes what God allocates to each of us; the combination of our distinctively designed hearts with our subsequent desires (motives) and our resources. Our hearts are unique (see Psalm 139). Our desires are unique (see Psalm 37:4). Our gifts, or our resources, are unique (see 1 Corinthians 12:4-6). God specifically orchestrates these so that we will serve the interests of others in an effort to reveal His grace and give Him glory (see 1 Peter 4:10). He holds us accountable to blamelessly steward our unique gifting (see Matthew 25:15). This exclusive talent is the one-of-a-kind expression of His story in us.

We are not to selfishly compare or contrast our circumstances with others, spending our time searching for and calling out inequities (see Galatians 6:4). After Jesus alluded to the tragic death that Peter would endure for his faith, He balked when His rocky disciple asked comparatively about what would happen to John. In essence, Peter was asking if Jesus would be fair. Jesus said: "If I want him to remain alive until I return, what is that to you? You must follow me" (John 21:22). Jesus was saying that the Creator determines what is fair and always considers the unique expression of His story in Peter, in John, and in each one of us. Individually, we are called to trust in the One who sees all things and is building His kingdom through us in fairness and equity.

At the same time, God is not giving us a one-for-one punishment for our sin (see Psalm 103:10). Nor is He divvying out tragedies onto people who are "worse sinners." He merely desires that we individually repent with all of our hearts, all of our desires, and all of our resources (see Luke 13:1-5) and surrender these to Him. In doing so, we are free to have blameless motives in interpersonal conflict.

Our internal motives, our innate self-interests, are oftentimes much closer than they at first appear—

—much like that message printed on your vehicle's rear-view mirror. Unfortunately, those motives are not always obvious because our perspective is skewed from selfishly comparing or contrasting our circumstances with others. When we spend too much time searching for inequities, our motives cannot be called blameless.

Inventory Your Motives

Are your motives blameless? Does interpersonal conflict cause you to first look toward your selfish interests, or do you approach that conflict selflessly, in the interests of others involved? During the next week, ask the Holy Spirit to help you inventory your motives whenever you find yourself in conflict. When two objects attempt to occupy the same space at the same time, let the Holy Spirit examine the selfishness or selflessness of your motives. When you uncover ignoble motives, humbly surrender them to God and ask His Spirit to move you from *selfish* to *selfless* (see Philippians 2:3). Then pursue the interests of the other parties involved in the conflict before your own, being careful to manage the conflict at hand toward solutions that are truly equitable.

INTIMACY WITH GOD

Third, "what is fair" includes *intimacy with God*—the connection of our innermost being with His. Solomon said: "For the crooked man is an abomination to the LORD; But He is intimate with the upright" (Proverbs 3:32 NASB). *Upright* refers to those who are fair. The New International Version translates this intimacy with God as being taken "into his confidence" (Proverbs 3:32). The King James Version says: "His secret is with the righteous" (Proverbs 3:32). The Amplified Bible Classic Edition references intimacy with God as "His confidential communion *and* secret counsel" (Proverbs 3:32).

The more intimate we are with God, the more we will work toward fairness in conflict. The more we work toward fairness in conflict, the more intimate we will be with God. This cycle changes how we measure the success of conflict management in our lives as we move from horizontal, competitive victory to knowing God more deeply and keeping His selfless perspectives in mind.

Through interpersonal conflict we can grow in our intimacy with God by doing all things through Christ who gives us strength (see Philippians 4:13). As we draw near to God, He draws near to us (see James 4:8). He never leaves or forsakes us (see Hebrews 13:5). He is our helper, freeing us from the fear of man (see Hebrews 13:6). In Christ, He understands our temptation to be unfair (see Hebrews 4:15). He allows us to endure only what temptation we can bear, always providing a way out (see 1 Corinthians 10:13). He comforts us (see 2 Corinthians 1:5). He matures us (see James 1:4). He gives us wisdom (see James 1:5). He develops our perseverance (see Romans 5:3). That perseverance produces character that gives us hope because we have intimacy with God through the indwelling of His Holy Spirit see (Romans 5:4-5). He works in all conflict for our "good" (Romans 8:28); *good* here is defined as His work to shape us to be like Christ (see Romans 8:29). Then He uses our intimacy with God to, through us, introduce Christ to others who are encountering similar trials (see 2 Corinthians 4:7-10; Philippians 1:12).

At least three avenues exist for us to increase our intimacy with God: the Word of God, the people of God, and the Spirit of God.

Get Intimate with God

How well do you know God? Are you familiar with His will, His mind, His emotions, and His Spirit? If you've decided to follow one of the reading plans outlined in the introduction to this book, single out one verse in Proverbs each morning, and meditate on it with God, applying those wise words to all of your tasks and appointments throughout the entire day. Pray for God's specific leading through this verse. If you're not following a reading plan, that's okay, but please do take the step of opening your Bible to the book of Proverbs and writing down one verse to think about throughout your day. Carry that verse with you and read it often. At the end of the day, take a few moments to reflect on what you learned about the heart of God through that verse. Do this for the next thirty days as you learn to search for fairness and equity in interpersonal conflict.

INTEGRITY

Fourth, what is fair includes *integrity*, the sense of being of one mind, complete and undivided. Solomon observed: "The integrity of the upright guides them, but the unfaithful are destroyed by their duplicity" (Proverbs 11:3). Once again, the "upright" are those whose paths are straight. When we are fair with others, we are guided by integrity. God calls us to be completely fair in all that we do, all of the time.

Too often we become "weary in doing good" (2 Thessalonians 3:13) after we have endured being fair for what we thought was a sufficient period of time. Weary from our efforts to look after the interests of other people, we finally see an opportunity where looking out for our own interests might provide immediate gain.

Often, we look at the other party involved in our conflict and see them as unfair, which helps us justify our own self-centeredness in return. In these cases, we become divided, or duplicitous, in our attempt at equity, and our integrity suffers.

In order to have the mind of Christ and work toward being completely fair in all of our dealings, we must pursue wisdom with all of our heart. Referencing the benefits of an all-out pursuit of wisdom, Solomon said: "Then you will understand what is right and just and fair—every good path" (Proverbs 2:9). God uses that pursuit in the midst of our conflict to complete us (see James 1:4). His wisdom prompts us to selflessly perceive what is fair (see Proverbs 8:6).

When it comes to being fair, integrity means that authority will equal responsibility. In other words, what we are in charge of must be equal to how we are held accountable. If we have a cell phone, we need to pay the bill.

Confess and Complete

We are called to love deeply, but differently. Equity means treating people fairly, but not the same. What about you? Are you completely fair to both sides whenever you experience conflict? Is there any conflict with a spouse, a child, a friend, a relative, a coworker, a customer, a vendor, a competitor, or even a fellow church member in which you have cut equity short? If so, confess and complete. Confess your shortfall to God, who will complete His work in you to be like Christ (see Philippians 1:6). Christ's work in you through the Holy Spirit will assist your attempts to find equity in your interpersonal or business conflicts.

QUESTIONS FOR REFLECTION

Think about your own concern for relational equity. When relational conflict occurs, do you only risk a little in an effort to win much more than you give? Do you create your own limited scale of what is fair? How do you feel when someone deals unfairly with you, and you wind up on the losing end?

Think about a recent conflict situation that you encountered. As you look back on it, can you discern what your motives were at the time? Did you first look toward your selfish interests, or did you approach that conflict selflessly, in the interest of the other people involved?

Can you gauge your intimacy with God? Doing so will help you to come at conflict with unselfish motives. How well do you know God? Are you familiar with His will, His mind, His emotions, and His Spirit?

Check your integrity when it comes to conflict. Are you completely fair to both sides whenever you experience conflict? Is there any conflict with a spouse, a child, a friend, a relative, a coworker, a customer, a vendor, a competitor, or even a fellow church member in which you have cut equity short and need to make amends?

How will your connection with God improve your fairness and equity in your conflict when it comes to your relationships? How can you make positive steps today to lean into God's concept of what's fair and allow him to be the judge?

WISDOM CHALLENGE

Read the Parable of the Workers in the Vineyard in Matthew 20:1-16. Ask yourself, honestly, do you think the vineyard owner acted with equity and fairness toward these hired workers? Discuss what kingdom values are represented here, and how those upside-down values characterize God's kingdom at work in your life. Then share what displaying such kingdom values might mean to the deepening of your relationships.

Chapter 6

Justice

How do you apply justice to your relationships when conflict has occurred? Our next pearl of wisdom is justice, (*mishpat* in Hebrew; see Proverbs 1:3). Whereas the pearl of righteousness precedes the adjustments made in conflict, and the pearl of equity is often applied during adjustments in conflict, the pearl of justice is most predominant after adjustments in conflict. The word *justice* comes from the Latin root word that means "lawful." The concept of justice applies to God's moral law, to our civil laws, to our organizational rules, and to our relational boundaries.

Justice is often represented using the image of scales. Solomon referenced how these scales affect those in the marketplace: "Honest scales and balances are from the LORD; all the weights in the bag are of his making" (Proverbs 16:11).

God tells us that justice is a paramount value for our relationships: "To do what is right and just is more acceptable to the LORD than sacrifice" (Proverbs 21:3).

In our study of Proverbs, we find that Solomon has uncovered four weights inside justice's measurement bag: *listening, equal opportunity, impartiality,* and *resolving conflict.* If we add to or subtract from one or more of these four weights, we elude justice in our relationships.

LISTENING

The first weight in the measurement bag of justice is: *listening.* Solomon wrote: "He who answers before listening—that is his folly and his shame" (Proverbs 18:13).

Listen to Others

When facing a conflict, your goal should be to *listen to others at least as much, if not more than, you speak.* If you are typically quick to speak, build a new habit of jotting down your thoughts while another person is speaking to you, rather than interrupting because you fear that you'll lose your train of thought. In order to accomplish true bidirectional listening, summarize what you're hearing and ask questions that reveal motives, interests, or desires while you maintain vertical sensitivity to the Holy Spirit. Maintain eye contact as well as heart contact, and use body language, facial expressions, and gestures that communicate understanding. While active horizontal listening repeats their words in yours, active vertical listening reveals His Word in yours.

EQUAL OPPORTUNITY

The second weight in the measurement bag of justice is *equal opportunity*. One of the biggest mistakes that we make in not bringing justice to our interpersonal conflict is acting on only one side of the story. Wisdom calls us to a more complete standard: "The first to present his case seems right till another comes forward and questions him" (Proverbs 18:17).

Get Both Sides of the Story

Keep your thoughts, choices, feelings, and prayers surrendered to the Holy Spirit. Wisely gather the rest of the story from all parties involved in the conflict. In doing so, do not betray confidence, do not condemn, and do not cut anyone short.

IMPARTIALITY

The third weight in the measurement bag of justice is *impartiality*. "It is not good to be partial to the wicked or to deprive the innocent of justice" (Proverbs 18:5; cf. 24:23).

Be Impartial

When it comes to interpersonal conflict, to you tend to be one-sided? Do you favor a particular kind of person or behavior over another? Do you find yourself either giving or receiving relational bribes? Have you ever allowed a corrupt witness to sway your judgment without carefully weighing both sides of the issue? If so, you are adding to or subtracting from justice's measurement bag in order to receive more for less or to deliver less for more. Each day during the next month, read Solomon's Psalm of Justice—Psalm 72. Let the words sink into your soul, allowing them to assimilate into your life. This will enhance impartiality in your interpersonal conflicts, as the presence of Christ in you brings justice to your relationships.

CONFLICT RESOLUTION

The fourth weight in the measurement bag of justice is *conflict resolution*. "There is deceit in the hearts of those who plot evil, but joy for those who promote peace" (Proverbs 12:20). Justice, or true conflict resolution, promotes peace. "By justice a king gives a country stability, but one who is greedy for bribes tears it down" (Proverbs 29:4).

Resolve Conflict

Are you characterized and known as a person who leaves conflict unresolved? Do you have strife in your life because unresolved conflict is lingering in any of your relationships? Is there a friend or a sibling that you haven't spoken to for years because of this? Pray for the Holy Spirit's guidance; read the aforementioned verses relating to resolving conflict; seek wise counsel; and then, if possible, as far as it depends on you, wisely resolve the conflict to restore the relationship.

Christ is the *justice* of God, and we humbly integrate His justice into our lives by faith (see Romans 3:25-26). Jesus fulfilled the Old Testament Law, clarifying that God established that law to point toward the restoration that he would bring (see Matthew 5:17). God the Father sent Jesus into the world to proclaim justice to the nations (see Matthew 12:18; cf. Isaiah 42:1). Jesus was innocent, yet He was condemned to bring justice and mercy in order to free the guilty (see 1 Peter 3:18). When we humble all four chambers of our heart to God, He brings justice to our relationships through the person of Christ so that we can navigate through conflict to community. Only through Him do we experience what is actually intended as we value listening, equal opportunity, impartiality, and conflict resolution in our everyday lives.

QUESTIONS FOR REFLECTION

Do you practice true bidirectional listening? Try using the strategies described above: Summarize what you're hearing and ask questions that reveal motives, interests, or desires while you maintain vertical sensitivity to the Holy Spirit. Maintain eye contact as well as heart contact, and use body language, facial expressions, and gestures that communicate understanding. Go ahead, try these strategies and see how they work!

When in a conflict situation, do you listen long enough so that you don't act on only one side of the story? How does a failure to listen affect the outcome of any conflict situation? What are the benefits to listening closely and asking the right questions?

When it comes to interpersonal conflict, to you tend to be one-sided? Do you favor a particular kind of person or behavior over another? Have you ever allowed a corrupt witness to sway your judgment without carefully weighing both sides of the issue? What are the outcomes of having this kind of a one-sided perspective in conflict?

Do you prefer to avoid conflict? Do you have strife in your life because unresolved conflict is lingering in any of your relationships? Is there a friend or a sibling that you haven't spoken to for years because of this? What might happen if you spoke to that person and resolved the conflict?

How is maintaining a close connection to God beneficial to understanding the causes of justice that He's concerned about? Is there some local organization that you could support with your time, talent, and treasure that would help, even in some small way, to begin to alleviate injustice in someone's life?

WISDOM CHALLENGE

Read the Parable of the Sheep and the Goats in Matthew 25:31-46. This picture of the end times is a vivid reminder that injustice exists in the world and that Christians are called to do something about it. Discuss what this passage means for the kinds of justice issues that God is passionate about, and talk about ways that active listening, getting both sides of the story, remaining impartial, and engaging with others in calling for justice can help to build God's kingdom on the earth. Decide as an individual or as a group on one concrete way that you can start to alleviate injustice both in your personal communication and in your larger community.

Chapter 7

Wise Behavior

In conflict management, is your behavior wise or foolish? A key indicator of the answer to this question lies in how we utilize the Bible's teachings when two objects attempt to occupy the same space at the same time in our lives. Proverbs demonstrates a direct correlation between wise behavior in conflict management and how we assimilate the Word of God into our lives.

One of the main purposes of Proverbs is to give the reader instruction in wise behavior (see Proverbs 1:3 NASB). The mystery of wise behavior perpetuates effective communication into the power of persuasion. It delves into the unseen, bringing wisdom into the hearts of others.

In the book of Proverbs Solomon pleaded: "My son, do not forget my teaching, but keep my commands in your heart, for they will prolong your life many years and bring you prosperity. Let love and faithfulness never leave you; bind them around your neck, write them on the tablet of your heart. Then you will win favor and a good name in the sight of God and man" (Proverbs 3:1-4). "A good name" is translated from the same root as the Hebrew word for "wise behavior" (*sakal*). When we learn wisdom, it sinks deep into our hearts and becomes evident in our actions. This leads to wise behavior that is demonstrated both vertically and horizontally.

Whereas someone who practices foolish behavior trusts in their own words, which tend to be unconvincing, nonsensical, fearful, and lacking credibility, someone who practices wise behavior acts in the opposite manner by trusting in and following the Word of God.

Proverbs tells us that wise behavior has four characteristics: it is *convincing*, *common sense*, *courageous*, and *credible*. Jesus' life was characterized and known by these four traits.

CONVINCING

First, wise behavior is *convincing*. This persuasiveness comes from our speech. To be convincing with our words, we must first have wisdom in our hearts. Solomon taught: "The heart of the wise instructs his mouth, and adds persuasiveness to his lips" (Proverbs 16:23 NASB). Proverbs precedes this verse with: "He who gives attention to the word will find good, and blessed is he who trusts in the LORD" (Proverbs 16:20 NASB). The word translated "attention" is derived from the same Hebrew word as *wise behavior*. When we give attention to wise instruction, we begin to become convincing in our speech. Our most powerful source of wise instruction is, of course, the Word of God.

When our words are filled with the Word, we are convincing.

Be Convincing

Take a journey upward in order to change inwardly. Memorize a verse or passage from Proverbs. Allow wise behavior to sink into your heart through the power of the Word.

COMMON SENSE

Second, wise behavior includes *common sense*. Solomon said that the fool lacks this commodity (see Ecclesiastes 10:3). To have common sense, we must apply Scripture to our lives. To "apply" carries the sense of "to make sticky." Wise behavior makes the Word "sticky" to our lives. The result of that kind of stickiness is common sense.

Wise behavior applies the Word of God to our work. Solomon wrote: "He who gathers crops in summer is a wise son, but he who sleeps during harvest is a disgraceful son" (Proverbs 10:5). Working smart by integrating the Word into life is common sense.

Wise behavior applies the Word of God to our communication. Solomon said: "When words are many, sin is not absent, but he who holds his tongue is wise" (Proverbs 10:19). Using restraint is common sense.

Wise behavior also applies the Word of God to our choice of an audience. Solomon said: "Do not speak to a fool, for he will scorn the wisdom of your words" (Proverbs 23:9). Avoiding conversation with a fool is common sense.

Wise behavior applies the Word of God to our perspective. Following this line of thinking, Solomon taught: "A man's wisdom gives him patience; it is to his glory to overlook an offense" (Proverbs 19:11). Overlooking an offense is common sense.

Wise behavior applies the Word of God to our pursuit of intimate relationships. Solomon observed: "Houses and wealth are inherited from parents, but a prudent wife is from the LORD" (Proverbs 19:14). "Prudent" is translated from the same Hebrew word that is translated "wise behavior." Listening to a wife whose behavior is wise is common sense.

Be Filled with Common Sense

Look at your calendar with your memorized words of wisdom in mind. Ask God how you can apply this wise behavior to your everyday life. Inspire the people you work and live with as you approach every interaction with God's common sense.

COURAGEOUS

Third, wise behavior is *courageous*. To be courageous, we must be willing to share our experience of the Word with another person. Solomon taught: "When a mocker is punished, the simple gain wisdom; when a wise man is instructed, he gets knowledge" (Proverbs 21:11).

Be Courageous

Share with someone your experience of applying a selected verse or passage to your life. That person will be honored that you are courageous enough to open up to them about the changes God is working out in your life.

CREDIBLE

Finally, wise behavior is *credible*. To be credible, we must give credit to God for our experience of getting into the Word, applying it to our lives, and being courageous enough to share that experience with another person. Solomon observed: "A man is praised according to his wisdom, but men with warped minds are despised" (Proverbs 12:8). "Wisdom" is translated from the same Hebrew word for "wise behavior" that Solomon noted as praiseworthy or credible.

Be Credible

We can pray that our friends will also be drawn to repentance toward God through our wise behavior consisting of *convincing words*, *common sense*, *courage*, and *credibility*. Jesus Christ, the Wisdom of

God (see 1 Corinthians 1:24), through His life, death, and resurrection, demonstrated God's ultimate design for wise behavior. Jesus was *convincing:* He knew the Word. Jesus was filled with *common sense:* He applied the Word. Jesus was *courageous:* He shared the Word. Jesus was *credible:* He died for the Word, giving all credit to the Father. Jesus Christ was and is still today the Word of God. Thus, it is Christ in us who is *convincing*, filled with *common sense, courageous*, and *credible*. When people ask more about your experience with memorizing, applying, and sharing the Word of God, give credit to Him.

QUESTIONS FOR REFLECTION

Have you learned to integrate the wisdom of the Scriptures into your life? Proverbs is absolutely packed with practical wisdom that you can bring into your conflict situations.

Have you integrated the Word of God into your life so that you can practically apply it to conflict situations? Read Proverbs 1 and think about one situation in your life where you can directly apply the wisdom in this chapter.

Have you ever told another person about how your experience with Scripture has changed your perspective? Consider how a courageous conversation with another person could change their perspective on a troublesome situation in their life.

Is the Word of God evident in your life to the point where other people have asked you where your peace or wisdom comes from? If so, be certain to give credit to God.

How do you engage with Scripture on a regular basis? Make it a goal to begin to find a place and a time to do so and discuss with others the ways that they have found to integrate the Word into their lives.

WISDOM CHALLENGE

Read Stephen's beautiful testimony in Acts 7:1-60. Analyze how he embodied the principles in this chapter and the Word of God to be courageous, convincing, use common sense, and be credible in the face of his accusers. When you read how the Jewish leaders reacted, also consider how the truth of God's Word could potentially impact your testimony to others.

Chapter 8

Understanding

The next pearl for wise conflict management is understanding, noted in Solomon's purpose for writing Proverbs, which is "understanding words of insight" (Proverbs 1:2). Understanding occurs through an intimate experience with the Holy Spirit who gives us insight into others: "The fear of the LORD is the beginning of wisdom, and knowledge of the Holy One is understanding" (Proverbs 9:10). In order to be understanding, we must be *Spirit-led, teachable, cool,* and *insightful*.

SPIRIT-LED

Proverbs tells us that a person with understanding is plugged into and *led* by the Holy Spirit. Solomon said: "Knowledge of the Holy One is understanding" (Proverbs 9:10). In order to be understanding, we must first trust in the Spirit of God with all of our hearts.

The determining factor in testing whether we are Spirit-led is the Five-Second Rule: taking five seconds before every telephone call, text, email, encounter, or meeting to ask the Holy Spirit, "What do you want me to do in this situation?" This focuses our hearts on trusting the heart of God, who gives us the power to selflessly listen and understand the hearts of others.

What about you? When your spouse speaks with a discouraging tone, take five seconds to ask God, "What do you want me to do?" When someone cuts you off on the highway, take five seconds to ask God, "What do you want me to do?" When a co-worker or teammate lashes out at you, take five seconds to ask God, "What do you want me to do?" When you are in the midst of a presentation and you're asked a tough question, take five seconds to ask God, "What do you want me to do?" When you're in the fray of a sports competition with the game on the line, take five seconds and ask God, "What do you want me to do?" When any temptation lurks before you, take five seconds to ask God, "What do you want me to do?"

Remain Plugged in to the Holy Spirit

Live by the Five-Second Rule. Before every telephone call, text, email, encounter, or meeting, ask the Spirit of God to lead you. Before you speak any words or take any actions, ask Him, "What do you want me to do?"

TEACHABLE

Second, in order to have understanding, we must be *teachable*. Solomon said that a person with understanding opens the door of his heart to a teacher in his life who will coach and correct him: "He who ignores discipline despises himself, but whoever heeds correction gains understanding" (Proverbs 15:32).

To gain understanding, we must employ the Times-Two Rule, which involves recruiting a teacher.

Remain Teachable

Live by the Times-Two Rule by asking someone to coach you in an arena of your life where you can grow in understanding. Find someone who is wiser than you in that selected discipline. Meet at least once each month to pursue specific areas of improvement.

COOL

Third, Proverbs says that a person with understanding has a *cool* spirit: "He who restrains his words has knowledge, and he who has a cool spirit is a man of understanding" (Proverbs 17:27 NASB). Being cool helps us avoid misunderstandings by helping us to remain silent, patient, and on a straight path.

A person with understanding keeps cool in conflict by knowing when to remain silent. "A man who lacks judgment derides his neighbor, but a man of understanding holds his tongue" (Proverbs 11:12).

Silence is cool.

A person with understanding keeps cool in conflict by remaining patient. "A patient man has great understanding, but a quick-tempered man displays folly" (Proverbs 14:29).

Patience is cool.

A person with understanding keeps cool in conflict by remaining on a straight path. "Folly delights a man who lacks judgment, but a man of understanding keeps a straight course" (Proverbs 15:21).

Straight is cool.

The Ten-Second Rule reminds us that in the heat of the moment we should invest ten full seconds to take our anger to God. He will cool us down, keeping us silent, patient, and on the straight path.

Stay Cool

Practice the real Ten-Second Rule. Take your anger to God. As you begin to heat up, ask Him to cool you down keeping you silent, patient, and following a straight path. Think about the potential impact of silence, patience, and following a straight course when you take a step back, relax your facial expression, make eye contact, demonstrate an engaging body posture, and use appropriate gestures to cool a conflict. This is just one way that you will experience Christ working through you.

INSIGHTFUL

Fourth, Proverbs teaches that a person with understanding is *insightful:* "The purposes of a man's heart are deep waters, but a man of understanding draws them out" (Proverbs 20:5). Understanding allows us to look into and reach inside another person's mind and heart, making us insightful.

We learn how to be insightful when we employ the Twenty-Second Rule: Take twenty seconds after each conversation to look past a person's words and into his or her heart. During this time you can examine the choices, thoughts, prayers, and feelings that comprise the source of his or her desires, or motives.

Language is only symbolic of the heart. Consequently, the words a person speaks often do not accurately reflect his or her heart. After being Spirit-led with the Five-Second Rule, being teachable through the Times-Two Rule, and being cool through the Ten-Second Rule, we can be insightful through the Twenty-Second Rule.

Pursue Insight into Other People

Live by the Twenty-Second Rule. Take twenty seconds after each conversation to look past every person's words in order to peer inside his or her heart. Don't merely focus on their vocabulary, but reflect on what resides in their heart that they were attempting to describe. Be a wise person who understands others by intimately experiencing the Holy Spirit. Be Spirit-led through the Five-Second Rule, teachable with the Times-Two Rule, cool while implementing the Ten-Second Rule, and insightful while engaging in the Twenty-Second Rule. Memorize the Bible verse in this chapter that seems most applicable to your life so that you can begin to assimilate understanding into your life through the Holy Spirit. He will equip you to wisely minimize misunderstandings in your conflict management.

QUESTIONS FOR REFLECTION

Have you ever considered using something like the Five-Second Rule in your own life? What do you think it would do to your conflict situations to ask God what He wants you to do before making a move? Five seconds is all it takes, and then listen for His response in your spirit.

Do you have in mind a person who could help you with the Times-Two Rule that says that you're twice as effective when you have a mentor who can show you the ropes? Consider approaching this person within the next week to ask about a mentorship plan. Then consider who you could also mentor in the spiritual life.

How do you think the Ten-Second Rule could help to defuse a heated conversation? Are you willing to use this the next time you become angry, giving your emotions to God and letting Him be the judge?

After having a conversation with another person, are you willing to use the Twenty-Second Rule to evaluate that person's thoughts and motives after the fact? Can you see what kind of impact there would be to doing something like this?

The overall thrust of this chapter is an emphasis on tapping in to God's Spirit and being patient. Write down one way that you can be Spirit-led with the Five-Second Rule, teachable through the Times-Two Rule, cool through the Ten-Second Rule, and insightful through the Twenty-Second Rule.

WISDOM CHALLENGE

Read the story of Daniel's faithfulness in Daniel 6:1-28. See especially verse 10, where it describes Daniel going home to pray immediately upon hearing about King Darius' decree that people only worship him. Discuss how Daniel's daily practice of praying to God despite his circumstances benefitted him in his daily walk. The only proof you need for the benefits of patiently turning to God is a look at Daniel 4:28.

Chapter 9

Wise Communication

The art of the well-asked question provides a disarming environment. It helps a difficult person to feel less threatened, which allows him to engage his heart while attempting to answer the inquiry. Solomon articulated the power of a question to generate answers when he wrote: "The first to present his case seems right, till another comes forward and questions him" (Proverbs 18:17).

Do you ever struggle with engaging a challenging person during interpersonal conflict? Do you feel like your hard-hearted counterpart does not listen to your statements? In conflict are you a person who tells, or are you training to be a person who ASKS?

The four components of being a person who ASKS include: *Ask questions*, *Share stories*, *Key in on the other person's perspective*, and *Speak Scripture*.

Proverbs describes an emerging leader who uses wise communication in one of its twelve purposes: "For understanding proverbs and parables, the sayings and riddles of the wise" (Proverbs 1:6). A saying is best delivered in the form of a question. A parable shares a story. A riddle keys in on another person's perspective. A proverb is wisdom from Scripture.

Wise conflict management prioritizes understanding riddles, including proverbs and parables as well as sayings of the wise, in order to use the four components of a person who ASKS to communicate effectively with others.

ASK QUESTIONS

When presented with challengers, Jesus asked questions (see Luke 20:1-8; Matthew 21:23-27).

Ask Questions that Engage the Heart

Rather than falling into the temptation to make harsh or stern statements that produce resistance during conflict, ask sincere questions that provide an environment and process for your challenger to peer inward and generate answers.

SHARE A STORY

The second word in our ASKS acronym involves the following concept: When you're locked in conflict, share a story that opens the meaning of the truth you're trying to communicate to the other person. Jesus shared stories with those who challenged Him in order to help them see His heart, their own hearts, and the hearts of others (see Luke 20:9-19; Matthew 22:1-14). Jesus told stories to keep people open to His message, understanding that truth discovered is vastly more powerful for learning than truth merely presented (see Matthew 13:10-17).

Become a Storyteller

Open the truths you're trying to communicate to your listeners in a personal way. When experiencing interpersonal conflict, use stories to communicate how you choose, think, pray, or feel. Allow your hard-hearted counterpart the opportunity to discover the truth you are communicating as you resist the temptation to hard-heartedly present that same truth.

KEY IN ON THE OTHER PERSON'S PERSPECTIVE

The third word in our ASKS acronym involves *keying in on the other person's perspective* with a thought-provoking question that engages his mind and exposes his heart.

Two thousand years ago, Jesus looked at the hearts of His detractors—spies who had been sent by the teachers of the law and the chief priests. These undercover agents had pretended to be honest, using flattery to trap the Son of Man with questions designed to trip Him up so that they could hand Him over to the power and authority of the governor. Nestled in their pockets was a denarius, a coin worth about a day's wages that featured the image of the emperor Tiberius and an inscription boasting his deity, "Tiberius Caesar, Augustus, son of the divine Augustus." Both the image and the statement would have been repulsive to the Jews living under Roman occupation. After gaining their perspective on the question at hand, Jesus not only exposed the coin, but also their hearts, through the shrewd use of a puzzle involving a thought-provoking question (see Luke 20:20-26; Matthew 22:15-22).

Key in on Your Detractor's Perspective

First, ask the Holy Spirit for insight into the perspective of your challenger's heart and his subsequent desires. Second, ask the Holy Spirit to give you a thought-provoking question that will help uncover his hardness of heart.

SPEAK SCRIPTURE

The last part of the ASKS acronym is to *speak Scripture*, humbly applying it to your role in the conflict. When the Sadducees, who did not believe in the resurrection, challenged Jesus, He used the authority of Scripture to bring truth to the conflict (see Luke 20:27-39; Matthew 22:23-33, 34-40).

Humbly Present Truth

Apply the truth of the Bible to your role in the conflict, rather than using it to pound your challenger. This will help you to avoid perpetuating pretense. Bring wise communication to your wise conflict management and experience the power of four communication components evidenced in the life of Christ. When encountering a challenging person during interpersonal conflict, train to be a person who ASKS, rather than a person who tells.

First, *ask questions* that engage the heart. Remember that questions generate answers and statements produce resistance.

Second, *share a story* that opens up the truths you're trying to communicate.

Third, *key in on the other person's perspective* with a thought-provoking question that engages his mind and exposes his heart. Ask the Holy Spirit for insight into the perspective of your challenger's heart and his subsequent desires. Next, ask the Holy Spirit to give you a thought-provoking question that will help uncover your challenger's hardness of heart.

Fourth, *speak Scripture*, humbly applying its truth to your role in the conflict, rather than using it to pound your challenger and advancing pretense.

Christ in you will provide wise communication in the midst of your conflict.

QUESTIONS FOR REFLECTION

When approaching a conflict situation, do you ask questions to get to the heart of the matter? How can you integrate this discipline in your life?

It may seem natural, but when you're conversing with others, do you find it easy to share a story about yourself or about another person that will help them see a deeper perspective? Can you think of a conversation recently where you shared from your own life experience?

What do you think of the goal of being more perceptive when it comes to your opponents in conflict? Are you willing to ask the Spirit to inspire you to ask a question, as Jesus often did, to change the focus of the discussion and reveal the deeper truths of their hearts?

Are you willing to be teachable and apply the words of Scripture regarding your personal humility and thinking of the other person first in your next conflict situation? How might this perspective have impacted one of your most recent conflicts?

How do you think wise communication, as outlined in this chapter, can have an impact in your life?

WISDOM CHALLENGE

Read the story of Samson posing a riddle to the people at his wedding party in Judges 14:1-20. Discuss how the riddle exposed the intentions of these supposed friends and also how Samson's new wife reacted when he refused to tell her the answer. Read to the end of the chapter to discover how God's Spirit helped him to react and respond after the riddle's answer was exposed. Despite the graphic detail, consider how using similar language in your conflict situations will be beneficial to exposing the motives behind other people's intentions in conflict.

Chapter 10

Prudence

In order to wisely manage interpersonal conflict, we must learn to master the pearl of prudence. Solomon held up prudence as one of the key purposes of his book of Proverbs: "for giving prudence to the simple" (Proverbs 1:4). Where we find wisdom, we find prudence (see Proverbs 8:12).

Prudence can be defined as "being both shrewd and innocent." When sending His disciples to advance the news of the kingdom of heaven amid what He knew would be challenging interpersonal conflict for those men, Jesus said: "I am sending you out like sheep among wolves. Therefore be as shrewd as snakes and as innocent as doves" (Matthew 10:16).

When we examine its contextual usages in Proverbs, we see four shrewd and innocent patterns of prudence: *ignore insults, foresee danger, be informed,* and *do not flaunt knowledge*.

IGNORE INSULTS

Solomon taught: "A fool shows his annoyance at once, but a prudent man overlooks an insult" (Proverbs 12:16).

Hand Over Insults to God

At work in each person who fires insults is a combination of dissatisfied desires. They are out of control, insecure, discontent, and insignificant from trusting in their perceived giftedness, rather than their actual godliness. The more they pursue satisfaction of their desires apart from God, the more dissatisfied they become. However, we need to be careful because that same pride is at work in us. When insulted, we are tempted to retaliate and make threats. That's why we need to learn that it's wise to ignore an insult.

Pride comes at conflict from the top down and results in foolishness, but humility comes from the bottom up and offers wisdom. When the wolves of conflict insult you, ignore them. Don't retaliate. Don't make threats. Instead, hand them over to God, and deflect the demeaning words with your shield of faith.

FORESEE DANGER

The second part of prudence is that, when encountering the wolves of conflict, we must *foresee danger*. Rather than speed blindly ahead into our own fallen reactions, we are called to exercise foresight into the potential danger lying ahead in our steps, our pathway, and our destination of conflict management.

Prudence foresees the danger of simple steps. Solomon warned of gullibility in interpersonal conflict: "A simple man believes anything, but a prudent man gives thought to his steps" (Proverbs 14:15).

Prudence foresees the danger of a deceptive pathway. When we foresee danger, we look forward to the pathway where our next steps lead. This includes the consequences of both our words and our actions. Solomon advised: "The wisdom of the prudent is to give thought to their ways, but the folly of fools is deception" (Proverbs 14:8).

Prudence foresees the danger of a suffering destination. When we foresee danger, we look forward to the destination of our conflict management—its effect on the relationship. It will be one of either suffering or safety. Solomon observed: "A prudent man sees danger and takes refuge, but the simple keep going and suffer for it" (Proverbs 22:3; cf. 27:12).

Discern Your Steps

When you encounter the wolves of conflict, foresee the danger in your steps, your pathway, and your destination. Ask God if your steps are simple or prudent, if your pathway is deception or integrity, and if your destination is suffering or safety. If you discern that His Spirit is prompting you to see your steps as simple, and therefore inadvisable, then exchange those steps for prudent ones.

BE INFORMED

The third aspect of pursuing prudence when encountering the wolves of conflict is that we must *be informed*. Solomon referred to this information as knowledge, which we saw earlier as an intimate experience—the connection of our innermost being with God. Solomon wrote: "Every prudent man acts out of knowledge, but a fool exposes his folly" (Proverbs 13:16). Prudence flows from knowledge, yet the more we act with prudence, the more knowledge we receive.

Ask, Listen, Learn, and Lean

What about you? Are you asking, listening to, learning from, and leaning on the Spirit of God so that you can engage the same way in your relationships? When we are informed vertically, God equips us to be informed horizontally. When you encounter the wolves of conflict, ask prudent questions of God and of others. Then listen to, learn from, and lean on your heavenly Father. The intimate connection you'll experience with His Spirit will allow you to act with prudence.

DO NOT FLAUNT KNOWLEDGE

The fourth aspect of following a life of prudence is that, when encountering the wolves of conflict, we *do not flaunt knowledge*. Only fools tell all they know. Solomon cautioned: "A prudent man keeps his knowledge to himself, but the heart of fools blurts out folly" (Proverbs 12:23).

Don't Tell All You Know

When you encounter the wolves of conflict, resist the temptation to tell all you know. Do not use information to criticize others or flatter yourself. Ask the Holy Spirit to guide you in the discernment of what shrewd and innocent words to say. When we master prudence, it is not merely we who are advancing the kingdom of heaven amidst challenging interpersonal conflict; rather, it is Christ in us.

QUESTIONS FOR REFLECTION

One of the difficult parts of this section on prudence is in ignoring insults. How can you strategize to ignore the insults of one who wants to distract you into making a poor decision? Discuss how one might do something like this in a practical way.

What is one way you can learn to foresee danger in conflict, to learn from past conflicts, and to perceive the outcomes of wise actions versus foolish actions as you address another person in a conflict situation?

Think about how you typically are in a conflict situation. Are you calm enough to ask questions that are Spirit-led to make sure that you're understanding all the aspects of the conflict before you move forward?

Discuss the benefits of holding back information in a particular conflict situation. Often, it is tempting to come at someone with both barrels blazing so that you can make your argument, but consider how holding back might be beneficial to the overall discussion.

Can you explain in one sentence what being shrewd and innocent means to you? How will following Jesus' example in this way help you as you face future conflict?

WISDOM CHALLENGE

Read the Parable of the Shrewd Manager in Luke 16:1-15. Discuss the shrewd nature of the manager's actions after the rich man took away his job. This is a difficult parable to discuss, but dig deep. How did his actions of asking questions, foreseeing danger, understanding his situation, and withholding knowledge from his master dovetail with what you learned in this chapter? Why did the rich man commend him? Be sure to read Jesus' words to the Pharisees at the end of the passage and discuss what His admonitions meant in the context of this parable.

Chapter 11

Discretion

The word discretion means "to separate." Proverbs tells us that during interpersonal conflict, we need to introduce the air of the Holy Spirit's wisdom so that we can separate what is valuable from what is vulnerable. This Spirit of Christ allows what is valuable, the cream, to rise to the top. Without discretion, our lives, our relationships, and our efforts to manage conflict will spoil: foolishness will spoil wisdom; actions will spoil words; short-term pleasure will spoil long-term benefits; what's wrong will spoil what's right. Consequently, we must ask ourselves this question: "When two objects attempt to occupy the same space at the same time in our lives, how will we separate the valuable from the vulnerable?" In essence, how will we allow the cream to rise to the top so that we do not let it all spoil? Wisdom's answer is this: by using discretion (see Proverbs 1:4). From Proverbs, we learn that discretion separates wisdom from foolishness, walk from talk, long-term benefits from short-term pleasure, and right from wrong.

SEPARATE WISDOM FROM FOOLISHNESS

First, discretion separates *wisdom from foolishness*. As he set the course for his collection of wise sayings, Solomon emphasized how the search for wisdom must be paramount in our lives in order for us to choose it. We cannot discern wisdom from foolishness if we cannot distinguish authentic wisdom from counterfeit wisdom when we see it.

My son, if you accept my words and store up my commands within you, turning your ear to wisdom and applying your heart to understanding, and if you call out for insight and cry aloud for understanding, and if you look for it as for silver and search for it as for hidden treasure, then you will understand the fear of the LORD and find the knowledge of God. For the LORD gives wisdom, and from his mouth come knowledge and understanding. He holds victory in store for the upright; he is a shield to those whose walk is blameless, for he guards the course of the just and protects the way of his faithful ones. Then you will understand what is right and just and fair—every good path. For wisdom will enter your heart, and knowledge will be pleasant to your soul. Discretion will protect you, and understanding will guard you. (Proverbs 2:1-11)

In order to discover wisdom, we must value it greatly. We must be willing to accept it, store it up, listen for it, apply our hearts to it, call for it, cry aloud for it, and pursue it as if we're searching for hidden treasure, understanding that it comes from God. His Spirit gives us discernment between wisdom and foolishness so that the cream of wisdom can rise to the top in our interpersonal conflict.

Begin a Journey of Discretion

Read Proverbs 11:22. Think of a beautiful girl from your high school years who lacked discretion—the ability to separate life's most valuable from its most vulnerable. Now think of someone who had less beauty on the outside, but lasting beauty on the inside. Who is more beautiful today? The ability to separate wisdom from foolishness begins with humility toward the Spirit of God, accompanied by an all-out pursuit of His heart intersecting with street smarts. Begin your journey of discretion, separating wisdom from foolishness, by storing up Scripture in your heart. Memorize one verse from the Bible, and let it sink into your heart as you apply it to your life.

SEPARATE WALK FROM TALK

Discretion also separates *walk from talk.* Solomon noted the wisdom behind discerning the difference between a person's walk and their talk, even when we may be the one demonstrating the inconsistency.

Wisdom will save you from the ways of wicked men, from men whose words are perverse, who leave the straight paths to walk in dark ways, who delight in doing wrong and rejoice in the perverseness of evil, whose paths are crooked and who are devious in their ways (Proverbs 2:12-15).

Weigh Words against Behavior

When you engage with another person and experience negative conflict—tension that includes at least one sinful option—begin to use discretion to separate that person's walk from his talk. Look past his words into his behavior and weigh the two. Ask the Holy Spirit to guide you in this process and help you to act accordingly. Let the cream rise to the top as you separate the valuable from the vulnerable.

SEPARATE LONG-TERM BENEFITS FROM SHORT-TERM PLEASURE

The third aspect in our look into discretion involves separating *long-term benefits from short-term pleasure*.

My son, pay attention to my wisdom, listen well to my words of insight, that you may maintain discretion and your lips may preserve knowledge. For the lips of an adulteress drip honey, and her speech is smoother than oil; but in the end she is bitter as gall, sharp as a double-edged sword. Her feet go down to death; her steps lead straight to the grave. She gives no thought to the way of life; her paths are crooked, but she knows it not. (Proverbs 5:1-6)

The consequences of short-term pleasure include long-term detriments. When we learn to discern the difference, we become adept at equating selfish short-term gain with long-term pain.

Separate Valuable from Vulnerable

Are you tempted to pursue some short-term pleasure? Compare the potential devastation that will come to your life with the long-term benefits that discretion offers: gained credibility in your community, deepened family relationships, trusted friendships, the ability to respond to ministry opportunities, strengthened marketplace productivity, whole assets, increased autonomy, and decreased economic burden. Ask a loving God to make clear which is best for you. Listen to His prompting to separate the valuable from the vulnerable.

SEPARATE RIGHT FROM WRONG

Fourth, discretion knows how to separate *right from wrong*. In the three thousand years since Solomon's writings, little about human nature has changed. Too often our culture finds it increasingly difficult to separate right from wrong. Read how Solomon described the benefits of discretion's protection as he juxtaposed right and wrong:

Then you will walk in the ways of good men and keep to the paths of the righteous. For the upright will live in the land, and the blameless will remain in it; but the wicked will be cut off from the land, and the unfaithful will be torn from it. (Proverbs 2:20-22)

Desire Deeper Perception

Fear the Lord. Humble your heart, your desires, and your time, talent, and treasure to God in order to wisely implement discretion between right and wrong. Operate by yielding to the judgment of His Spirit in you, rather than defaulting to your own fallen, inconsistent, and inequitable determination of what is right and wrong. Pray to God specifically to lead you to know the difference, whether you're in a conflict situation or not. On your own, you cannot reliably separate the valuable from the vulnerable; rather, the Spirit of Christ in you leads you to do this through His power and His wisdom.

QUESTIONS FOR REFLECTION

How can you separate wisdom from foolishness in your life and in the conflict situations that you face? Does the picture of the beautiful woman with no discretion connect with you as you think about your own reactions to the conflict in your life?

One of the difficult ideas in this chapter was separating walk from talk, even when it comes to ourselves. How do you foster that kind of perception when looking at another person, and that kind of honesty when it comes to looking at yourself? Self-justification can be a powerful tool to blind us. How can you avoid this in your own personal life?

Today's culture definitely does not value long-term benefits over short-term pleasure. How can you stem the tide of this influence in your own life when it comes to your personal, financial, ministry, family, or business decisions? The ideas in this section have long-range implications. Discuss the ways in which you value short-term gains over long-term benefits.

In the three thousand years since Solomon's writings, little about human nature has changed. Too often our culture finds it increasingly difficult to separate right from wrong. Talk about the implications of sin's effects on our culture and on our lives when it comes to discerning right from wrong.

Developing discernment is a valuable aspect of gaining wisdom. Discuss with your small group or with a trusted friend who demonstrates wisdom in their decisions how the four aspects of this chapter have combined to help them gain a life of wisdom. How does an intimate connection with the Holy Spirit play into this kind of wisdom?

WISDOM CHALLENGE

Read the story of how Jesus was tested in the wilderness in Matthew 4:1-11. How did Jesus, this early in His ministry, demonstrate discernment in the way He rebuffed the devil's attempts to make Him act in His own self-interest? Realize that Jesus, as fully human, was in a desperately weakened condition, and yet He still maintained the discernment that He needed to stand strong in the face of Satan's opposition. How did Jesus manage to separate wisdom from foolishness, walk from talk, long-term benefits from short-term pleasure, and right from wrong in this situation so that He could discern what was valuable from what was vulnerable?

Chapter 12

Wise Counsel

Where do you go for wise advice? Our next pearl of wisdom is wise counsel. Solomon noted its importance for us as we seek to make wise decisions: "A wise man will hear and increase in learning, and a man of understanding will acquire wise counsel" (Proverbs 1:5 NASB). The NIV translates *wise counsel* as "guidance." In essence, it is sound advice.

Solomon pointed to four pillars that undergird the pursuit of shrewd advice. Each one focuses on recognizing the heart of the person providing the information. Wise counsel is *guidance from the wise, absent from the wicked, success from the Lord*, and *sweet from a friend*.

GUIDANCE FROM THE WISE

First, wise counsel is *guidance from the wise*. In the battle of interpersonal conflict, we need the counsel of more than one confidante in order to experience success. Solomon advised: "For waging war you need guidance, and for victory many advisers" (Proverbs 24:6). If we do not seek wise counsel, we lose. King Solomon warned: "For lack of guidance a nation falls, but many advisors make victory sure" (Proverbs 11:14). Our best efforts to plan our way through conflict will fall short without the input of others. Solomon taught: "Plans fail for lack of counsel, but with many advisers they succeed" (Proverbs 15:22). He also communicated the wise way to plan for conflict management: "Make plans by seeking advice; if you wage war, obtain guidance" (Proverbs 20:18). The wise in heart seek wise counsel even when planning their approach to conflict management.

Seek Guidance from the Wise

In the midst of your conflict, seek wise counsel from more than one credible source—perhaps from a friend, family member, coworker, pastor, small group leader, business owner, or teacher. Resist the temptation to go it alone on autopilot as you maintain control of your own life. Then ask yourself and ask the Holy Spirit if the counsel you receive is consistent with the wisdom in the Scriptures. Finally, use the wise counsel to help you plan your approach to wise conflict management.

ABSENT FROM THE WICKED

Second, wise counsel is *absent from the wicked*. Solomon cautioned: "The plans of the righteous are just, but the advice of the wicked is deceitful" (Proverbs 12:5). The advice of the wicked is not wise counsel at all, but a trap. The bait lures us to follow and to bite, but hidden inside is a hook. A wicked counselor deceitfully hides the hook of the consequences of his selfish motives inside the bait of gratifying our own selfish desires.

Recognize and Refuse Deceit from the Wicked

When you are seeking advice, listen for self-serving clues embedded in the words of your chosen advisor. Next, filter the advice through wisdom's biblical grid to discern whether the counsel is actually deceit from the wicked. Then ask yourself if you are motivated solely by a selfish benefit to follow the tainted advice. If self-serving cues exist, refuse the deceitful counsel. Finally, seek the wise counsel of another trusted mentor. Remember, it never hurts to get a second opinion.

SUCCESS FROM THE LORD

Third, wise counsel is *success from the Lord*. Solomon preached: "There is no wisdom, no insight, no plan that can succeed against the LORD" (Proverbs 21:30). In seeking wise counsel, we must remember that the information we receive is merely advice.

In order to receive wise counsel from the Lord, we must become rapid Holy Spirit responders. Timing can be critical, so we must not wait when His prompting is clear.

Succeed with Wise Counsel from the Lord

Become a rapid Holy Spirit responder. When the Spirit tells you to do something, don't delay! Take every conflict to God in prayer and listen for His prompting. Verify whether the counsel you are receiving is from Him by determining its consistency with the Bible, wise counsel, and the life and teachings of Christ. When all three are in agreement with your discernment of the Holy Spirit's prompting, then follow the wise counsel from the Lord. When you humble your heart to His agenda for your life, He will work in all things for your good through the advancement of Christ in you (see Romans 8:28-29).

SWEET FROM A FRIEND

Fourth, wise counsel is *sweet from a friend*. Solomon illustrated: "Oil and perfume make the heart glad, so a man's counsel is sweet to his friend" (Proverbs 27:9 NASB). When we are experiencing interpersonal conflict, it is wise to seek the sweet wise counsel of a true friend who has our best interests at heart.

Taste the Sweet Wise Counsel from a Friend

Read the story of David and Jonathan recorded in 1 Samuel 20. During your next interpersonal conflict, seek the wise counsel of a friend like Jonathan who has your best interests at heart. Experience the benefit of sound advice from a person who not only knows you well, but who also is familiar with the Bible's wisdom as well as the heart of God. Use your friend's wise counsel, and taste the sweet success intended by your Creator. This insight comes from our wise Counselor, the Spirit of Christ, dwelling in us (see John 14:26).

QUESTIONS FOR REFLECTION

The first part of this chapter in the book examined Rehoboam's decision to pursue wise counsel. How can you learn from what Rehoboam experienced and apply it to your own life as it involves finding the right counsel for the decisions you make?

How are you at recognizing advice when it is self-serving or deceitful? How can you discern which is good and which is wicked advice? Can you think of a situation in your past where you followed the wrong kind of advice? What was the outcome of that action?

How do you discern the Holy Spirit's prompting in your life? In finding out whether the advice you're receiving aligns with God's wisdom, what steps do you take? How does that apply to your practical, everyday life?

Who is the one person you can go to for solid, wise advice—the person who knows you better than any other and who always has your best interests at heart? Take a moment to thank that person with a note, a text, or some other short communication this week.

Remember the early discussions we had about "the fool" in chapter 2 of this workbook. One of the characteristics of the hardened fool is that they are resistant to wise advice. How can you take steps in your life to be more open to the wisdom of others? On the other hand, do you impart helpful wisdom to others that comes from your relationship with God, or do you intervene where your advice is not needed or wanted? How can you be more responsible both in seeking and giving wise advice?

WISDOM CHALLENGE

Read the story of Moses seeking wise advice from his father-in-law Jethro in Exodus 18:1-27. What was his conundrum? What was the advice that Jethro gave him? How did he respond? How can you open yourself up to wise advice, as did Moses? How can you be one who sees a difficulty and then imparts wisdom from God, as did Jethro?

Chapter 13

Discipline

The next pearl of wise conflict management is discipline. Discipline and disciple share the same root word, meaning "learner." In order to be wise disciples, we must surrender ourselves—including our conflict—to God, in a way similar to an athlete surrendering his will to a coach.

God's wisdom empowers us to experience discipline. Proverbs is written "for attaining wisdom and discipline" (Proverbs 1:2), and "for acquiring a disciplined and prudent life" (Proverbs 1:3). Solomon taught that we should actually *love* discipline: "Whoever loves discipline loves knowledge, but he who hates correction is stupid" (Proverbs 12:1). In his theme verse of Proverbs, Solomon warned that only a fool would despise discipline (see Proverbs 1:7).

Race car drivers are among the most disciplined athletes in all of sports. Using an oval racecourse illustration, we see that Solomon's track of discipline has four turns: *teach, train, test,* and *transform.* Each turn must be carefully navigated, or discipline does not make a full lap of wise conflict management, and the result is relational wreckage (see Proverbs 5:23). Let's look at all four aspects of this in turn.

TEACH

Turn one is *teach*. This is defined as, "I do. You watch." During this process, something is inspired, modeled, and explained, and that something is retained. King Solomon believed that humility toward God was the first step of being teachable: "The fear of the LORD teaches a man wisdom, and humility comes before honor" (Proverbs 15:33). *Teach* is translated from the same Hebrew root word for *discipline.* Solomon revealed: "Instruct a wise man and he will be wiser still; teach a righteous man and he will add to his learning" (Proverbs 9:9).

Teach First by Being Teachable

Navigate turn one in Solomon's track of discipline by implementing, "I do. You watch." Inspire, model, and explain the discipline you would like to instill in your disciples. Select the right words at the right time with the right tone of voice. Like a coach, encourage and cheer for the people whom you teach, but also instill the discipline that comes from knowing Jesus Christ and His wisdom.

TRAIN

Turn two of discipline's oval track is *train*. This can be stated as, "I do. You help." Training equips disciples with the tools to be successful. Solomon wrote about the lasting benefit of establishing training early in the discipline process: "Train a child in the way he should go, and when he is old he will not turn from it" (Proverbs 22:6).

Equip Yourself and Others

Navigate turn two of Solomon's track of discipline: "I do. You help." Initiate an apprentice program with your children, your teams, and your employees. Allow them to help you in your chosen discipline so that they can assimilate what is inspired, modeled, and explained into transferrable skills, one step at a time. As you are training, develop drills to train your learners in the desired skill set.

TEST

Turn three in our oval of discipline is *test*. This can be summed up as, this is "You do. I help." Solomon instructed that discipline is a precious choice: "Choose my instruction instead of silver, knowledge rather than choice gold" (Proverbs 8:10). Continuing with the precious-metal imagery, Solomon observed: "The crucible for silver and the furnace for gold, but the LORD tests the heart" (Proverbs 17:3; 27:21). God tests us in order to refine us.

Embrace the Refining Process

Ask God to test your heart for impurities, or mixed motivations. When they arise, ask Him to remove them. In the same way, navigate your children, employees, and teams through turn three of Solomon's track of discipline, "You do. I help." Just as in sports the best test is a scrimmage, so as we navigate this turn with another we must hand the wheel to those who will eventually need to control their own course and take our place. Provide them with opportunities to fail. Do not panic when the impurities rise to the surface. Rather, rejoice that the refining process will continue the learning experience, and use it as an opportunity to work your way out of a job by instilling discipline.

TRANSFORM

Turn four in discipline's oval is *transform*, or correct, the impurities that rise to the top during the testing process. This can be summarized as, "You do. I watch." Solomon noted that correction is ineffective by using words alone: "A servant cannot be corrected by mere words; though he understands, he will not respond" (Proverbs 29:19).

Correct with a Heart of Love

Work yourself out of a job by implementing, "You do. I watch." Review your correcting process. Do you transform only after you teach, train, and test? Ask God if you have been harsh or lenient. Examine how you can best transform your children, employees, or teams through a wise combination of positive reinforcement, negative reinforcement, or punishment all preceded by teaching, training, and testing. All the while, transform with a heart of love in order to provide and protect those involved so that Christ the Refiner is seen in them.

As we navigate the race of life, we must fix our eyes on Christ (see Hebrews 12:1-2). At the same time, we must inhale and exhale the Word of God, our divinely inspired instrument for all four turns (see 2 Timothy 3:16). When we teach, train, test, and transform disciples, we will not be the ones nestled in the drivers' seats; rather, it will be Christ in us, and Christ in those that we teach, navigating the four turns of discipline.

QUESTIONS FOR REFLECTION

How does being teachable reflect in your attempts to teach others? How teachable are you? When someone comes in with the right word at the right time, are you open to hearing it?

Are you the kind of person who just wants to do a task your own way? Are you willing to have others come alongside you and learn from you? Think about ways you could mentor another person, either in your family or in your workplace, and then determine to move toward this kind of an activity, even in a small way.

Testing others is easy if you're a teacher; not so much if you're the parent of a toddler. Training has to be scaled based on the abilities of the learner. How do you test others to help them grow? Is this activity a source of frustration for you, or can you see the long-term benefits in this kind of a test? What might those be?

How can you transform another person's life with a heart of love? What does discipline look like when it happens lovingly? How has someone transformed your life in this way in the past?

This chapter is about discipline. Solomon talked about "loving discipline and instruction." Does this resonate with you? Think of a time when you needed discipline in your life, and someone came alongside you to teach, train, test, and transform you.

WISDOM CHALLENGE

Read Paul's exhortation to the Corinthian church regarding self-discipline in 1 Corinthians 9:24-27. As you break down his athletic imagery, think about someone training for a marathon or an athlete training for the Olympic Games. How do these ideas of the coach and the athlete apply to the discussion above? Discuss how Paul lived out this admonition in his own life.

Chapter 14

Knowledge

One of the twelve stated purposes of Proverbs was for giving knowledge to the young (see Proverbs 1:4). The Hebrew word for knowledge is daath, meaning the connection of two innermost beings, or intimacy. Knowledge strengthens our capacity to wisely and relationally manage conflict. Solomon taught: "A man of knowledge increases strength" (Proverbs 24:5b). Knowledge helps us to intimately navigate through conflict to community in our relationships. Solomon gave us four steps to wisely connect with the innermost part of the person with whom we are having conflict: surrender our conflict to God, seek the motives of the person involved, spell out our motives humbly and wisely, and solve the conflict by discovering common ground.

SURRENDER OUR CONFLICT TO GOD

Step one is to *surrender our conflict to God*. Solomon's theme verse of Proverbs says: "The fear of the LORD is the beginning of knowledge" (Proverbs 1:7). The "fear of the LORD" involves surrendering our motives, the person involved, the problem, and the outcome to God.

Surrender Your Conflict to God Through Prayer

Surrender your motives, the person involved, the problem, and the outcome. Ask God to shape your heart and desires to reflect His, giving you the knowledge for wise conflict management. Stop white-knuckling any selfish desires.

SEEK THE MOTIVES OF THE PERSON INVOLVED

Step two is to *seek the motives of the person involved.* Solomon wrote: "The heart of the discerning acquires knowledge; the ears of the wise seek it out" (Proverbs 18:15). We seek the motives of the person involved by asking and listening. Solomon taught: "Apply your heart to instruction and your ears to words of knowledge" (Proverbs 23:12). First, ask questions that search the innermost part of the person in order to open the door to the motives behind their words. For example, we might ask, "What do you really desire? Why?" The answer to the question "Why?" typically reveals their motives. Second, listen to the answers to your questions, which helps you reach in and connect with the innermost part of the person, namely their motives. Seeking to understand those motives shifts you from focusing on the outward person to exploring the inward thoughts and feelings of that person.

Ask and Listen

First, ask questions that reveal motives of the heart: "What do you desire? Why?" Second, listen to what motives the person is attempting to describe. Move from focusing on the outward nature to exploring the inward thought and emotions of you counterpart. Finally, beware of the fool; it might be you.

SPELL OUT MOTIVES HUMBLY AND WISELY

Step three is to *spell out our motives humbly and wisely* to the other person involved in our conflict. Solomon wrote: "The lips of the wise spread knowledge; not so the hearts of fools" (Proverbs 15:7). By first surrendering our conflict to God and seeking our counterpart's motives, we are then able to communicate our own pure motives to the other person with a humble heart and wise words that connect with their heart.

Speak Knowledge

Use restraint by keeping proud and foolish words in the dark so that you can experience knowledge. Solomon said that one who can spell out his motives humbly and wisely is rare and valuable: "Gold there is, and rubies in abundance, but lips that speak knowledge are a rare jewel" (Proverbs 20:15).

SOLVE THE CONFLICT BY DISCOVERING COMMON GROUND

Step four is to *solve the conflict by discovering common ground.* Solomon warned: "With his mouth the godless destroys his neighbor, but through knowledge the righteous escape" (Proverbs 11:9). To paraphrase, our words either build bridges or walls. Knowledge seeks and discovers common ground in both persons' motives in the interest of building bridges.

What about you? Do you build bridges or walls with your words and your nonverbal cues? How would your life change if you would focus on building bridges?

Use Words That Build Bridges

Explore the inner workings of the other person instead of focusing on their outward demeanor in the conflict. Don't be in a hurry to force someone into a manufactured "quick fix." Proceed with caution because Solomon offered us four caveats: beware of white-knuckling our selfish desires regarding the conflict (see Proverbs 22:12); beware of a fool; it might be you (see Proverbs 14:6-7); demonstrate a concern for the poor (see Proverbs 29:7); and do not be in a hurry (see Proverbs 19:2). When we experience an intimate connection with our counterpart in conflict, we won't be doing so alone; rather, we will be connecting through Christ in us.

QUESTIONS FOR REFLECTION

How willing are you to surrender the outcomes of your conflict situation to God in prayer? Think of one small conflict situation in which you can completely rely on God's goodness and justice to prevail. Now think of a larger one and discuss what your comfort level with that is.

What's the best way that you've learned to discern the motives of others involved in conflict situations? What kinds of questions are best to ask so that you can dig deeper and find out what's really at the heart of such a situation?

How can one learn to take a step back and discern what their own motives are in a situation? Are you open to having another person explore your motives and help you understand yourself better?

Are you a bridge-builder or a wall-builder when it comes to conflict? Building bridges takes planning, wisdom, skill, long-term vision and patience. How can you use these strategies to build a bridge with your counterpart in conflict?

Paul stated: "Do nothing out of selfish ambition or vain conceit, but in humility consider others better than yourselves. Each of you should look not only to your own interests, but also to the interests of the others" (Philippians 2:3-4). How can you apply this wisdom to your life, given what we've been discussing in this chapter?

WISDOM CHALLENGE

Read the account of Jesus raising Lazarus from the dead in John 11:1-44. Read especially His discussion with Martha in this situation. How did He take the time to discern her motives? How did He gently correct her? What were Jesus' goals in delaying his trip—in other words, why did He let His friend Lazarus die? What might Martha have been white-knuckling in this situation, and how did Jesus respond to this desire, even though it was a good one? Consider His quiet patience in this situation and then read the reactions of all involved when he brought Lazarus out from the tomb!

Chapter 15

Learning

We have two options for dealing with interpersonal conflict: We either protect our pride or learn in our humility. The final pearl for wise conflict management is learning. Solomon taught learning as one of the twelve purposes of Proverbs: "Let the wise listen and add to their learning" (Proverbs 1:5). Proverbs offers four insights to learning both for and from conflict. The "Thirty Sayings of the Wise" begin with four insights to learning: "Pay attention and listen to the sayings of the wise; apply your heart to what I teach, for it is pleasing when you keep them in your heart and have all of them ready on your lips. So that your trust may be in the Lord, I teach you today, even you" (Proverbs 22:17-19).

When it comes to learning, we must: pay attention; listen; apply our hearts to learning wisdom; and keep the wisdom in our hearts, ready on our lips. The purpose of learning wisdom is to lean on God (see Proverbs 22:19). We can remember these insights in four images: motivate with honey, dig like miners, soak like sponges, and store up His commands.

MOTIVATE WITH HONEY

Learning for Conflict

First, we must learn to pay attention (see Proverbs 22:17). *Pay attention* is translated from the original Hebrew for "bend the ear." Rabbis motivated their young students to pay attention by giving them a spoonful of honey before learning. In order to learn wisdom for conflict, we must motivate with honey, with our ears bent as we pay attention to our earthly sources of heavenly wisdom.

Learning from Conflict

In the midst of conflict, we either protect our pride and fail, or learn in our humility that begins with God as our object and succeed. Solomon observed vertical humility as the source of wisdom: "The fear of the LORD teaches a man wisdom, and humility comes before honor" (Proverbs 15:33). In order to humbly learn from our conflict, we must motivate like honey as we also bend our ears and humbly pay attention horizontally to our counterparts in conflict.

Pursue Development of Your Motivations

In order to learn wisdom *for* conflict, consider how to honestly understand your own motivations. To learn *from* conflict, ask yourself, "What motivates me in this conflict?" Next ask, "Are my motives consistent with God's wisdom?"

DIG LIKE A MINER

Learning for Conflict

Second, we must *dig like miners* and listen to wise sayings (see Proverbs 22:17). This means that we get into our Bibles and read a chapter each day in Proverbs. As we dig into the pages of the Scriptures, we mine for the wisdom that God offers through Solomon's writings. In order to dig like miners, we need to determine: where and how we dig.

Do we dig best in light or dark settings? Eating and drinking, or abstaining from both? Where are we most comfortable: in hot or cool settings? Where will we do our best learning: with loud background noise, through TV or music, or do we need quiet?

Next, how do we dig: with *what* (concrete) or *why* (abstract)? Concrete diggers search for facts, while abstract diggers seek ideas and theories. Some of us need to know *why* before we care to know *what*.

Learning from Conflict

We flesh out our desire to dig like miners in our conflict by listening to the other person involved. Solomon reflected: "The wise in heart are called discerning, and pleasant words promote instruction" (Proverbs 16:21).

Mine for Wisdom

To learn *for* conflict, get out your Bible and read a chapter each day in Proverbs. Dig for the wisdom

God offers through Solomon's writings. Determine where you dig best and whether you are a concrete or abstract digger. Knowing whether you dig for *what* or *why* enhances the probability that you will find the richness for which you are mining. In order to learn *from* conflict, listen to the other person involved.

SOAK UP LIKE A SPONGE

Learning for Conflict

Third, we must develop a system to retain the information we mine when reading the Bible so that wisdom soaks in to the fabric of our lives. This *soaking* system enhances retention by hanging the information we need to learn on something that we already know. Solomon advised: "Instruct a wise man and he will be wiser still; teach a righteous man and he will add to his learning" (Proverbs 9:9). To be effective, a soaking system should be: visual, imaginative, and active.

Learning from Conflict

In order to learn *from* conflict, we must observe our behavior as well as that of others in order to soak up wisdom. Proverbs notes that when our hearts soak up what we observe during conflict, we can say: "I applied my heart to what I observed and learned a lesson from what I saw" (Proverbs 24:32).

Develop a System

To learn *for* conflict, develop a system to remember a key verse or concept in Proverbs. Hang the new information on something that you already know. Make the system visual, imaginative, and active. Perhaps learn to create a mind map. If you are a sequential soaker, develop your system with order. Outline the order of what you are trying to remember before going deeper and adding to it. If you are a random soaker, then you can identify big ideas and proceed with adding the concepts that apply best to your situation. In order to learn *from* conflict, observe the behavior of all involved in the dispute, and apply your heart to soaking in and retaining wisdom.

STORE UP HIS COMMANDS

Learning for conflict

Fourth, we must *store up* the wise sayings we have learned and organize them for efficient recall. "Keep them in your heart and have all of them ready on your lips" (Proverbs 22:18). This occurs when we *soak* with the same method that we *recall*.

Consequently, we must determine how we recall what we learn. We recall by seeing, hearing, or doing. Soaking in the same manner that we recall enhances the learning process. For example, if we use images to soak, then we see the same images when we recall. If we use sounds to soak, then we hear those sounds when we recall. If we use action to soak, then we perform an action when we recall.

Next, we must determine whether we recall big or small concepts. If we recall big concepts, we are global thinkers. We remember the book title, maybe a few chapter titles, as well as the major concept. If we recall small concepts, we are analytical. We remember the parts better than the whole, details more than broad concepts. Recognizing what we recall equips us to develop a system to soak in the same style in which we recall. This compensates for our weaknesses in learning. For example, if we are analytical, we should outline the big ideas of a book by first scanning it so that we do not miss the main message, overlooking the forest for the trees.

Learning from Conflict

In order to learn *from* interpersonal conflict, we need to store up information that is shared during our conflicts. Solomon offered the following wisdom for our words: "A wise man's heart guides his mouth, and his lips promote instruction" (Proverbs 16:23). When we function as storehouses for wisdom, we promote learning for ourselves as well as for others.

Lean In

To learn *for* conflict, recall your memory verse or concept and apply it to your life. Whether you recall either big or small concepts by seeing, hearing, or doing, construct a system to help you soak and recall in the same way. In order to learn *from* conflict, warehouse the valuable information shared during times of interpersonal tension, retaining and recalling it in a fashion that allows you to communicate wisely.

We were designed to learn wisdom so that we would lean on God, rather than lean on ourselves, protecting our pride. Solomon summarized the purpose of learning wisdom: "So that your trust may be in the LORD" (Proverbs 22:19). Humility toward God is the beginning (see Proverbs 1:7; 9:10; 11:2; 22:4) and the end (see Proverbs 22:19) of wisdom. Consequently, we lean to learn, and we learn to lean.

Jesus Christ is the wisdom of God (see 1 Corinthians 1:24). He invites us to learn from Him because He is humble in heart (see Matthew 11:29). When we humbly accept His invitation, we begin new life as His disciples with His Spirit dwelling in us. Consequently, when we learn both *for* and *from* conflict, it is not merely we, but Christ in us doing so.

QUESTIONS FOR REFLECTION

In what ways is wisdom as sweet as honey to your taste? Discuss ways that you can motivate yourself to pursue wisdom like you would some delicious chocolate or whatever you crave. How could that kind of a craving for wisdom impact your life as it comes to conflict in the real world?

Discuss with a group or with a trusted friend the ways you engage with your Bible. When is it most effective for you to read and listen to what God is saying? How can you take that same study and turn it toward another person in conflict, using what you've learned to humbly pursue the other person's perspective?

Reread the suggested strategies for soaking up and remembering what you learn from God's word. Do you know whether you learn abstract concepts best or if you're a detail person? How can this learning style, which God made and built into you, enhance your understanding of Scripture?

Have you ever seen a well-organized warehouse? Understanding the basics of labeling and organizing your learning based on your learning style will help you be better able to recall what you learn. How can you begin to integrate this kind of an organization with just a few verses today?

This final chapter in the workbook is a call for practical methods of learning, remembering, and recalling. When it comes to learning, we must: (1) pay attention; (2) listen; (3) apply our hearts to learning wisdom; and (4) keep the wisdom in our hearts, ready on our lips. How has this chapter equipped you for this kind of activity based on how you learn? Discuss what your first step will be in integrating the wisdom you've learned.

WISDOM CHALLENGE

Read the story about Philip and the Ethiopian in Acts 8:26-39. Discuss how the Ethiopian's journey has been like your journey through this study guide and through the *Street Smarts from Proverbs* book. Have there been any passages that have confused you? Has the information in this book been helpful in either working out that confusion or in reinforcing your beliefs? The Ethiopian went on his way rejoicing, having found the wisdom he was searching for. It is our prayer that, in this book, you will have found the same reason for rejoicing.

Conclusion

Now that you have made the journey through the Street Smarts from Proverbs Study Guide, develop a system to memorize these amazing pearls of wisdom: righteousness, equity, justice, wise behavior, understanding, wise communication, prudence, discretion, wise counsel, discipline, knowledge, and learning. In doing so, you will dramatically increase the likelihood that you will apply them to your life, especially as you navigate through conflict to community.

Would you not only memorize and apply these twelve words and their traits, but also mentor someone else who will do the same? If we all respond affirmatively to the call to pursue God's wisdom, then we will be ready to be used by God to restore our world together as we navigate through conflict to community.

About the Authors

Mitch Kruse is host of the television program *The Restoration Road with Mitch Kruse*, which airs on sixty networks throughout the world, where he teaches the Bible through stories of restoration. Mitch's first book, Restoration Road, chronicles his story paralleled with Jesus' Parable of the Prodigal Son. Mitch also appears monthly on radio.

Mitch was the youngest licensed Realtor in the nation and the first person to sell a vehicle for a documented $1 million cash while he earned his Bachelor of Science degree in business administration from Indiana University. For seventeen years, Mitch Kruse was owner, CEO, and auctioneer of Kruse International, the world's largest collector-car sales organization. After selling his company to eBay, Mitch earned his Master of Arts and Doctor of Religious Studies degrees with high distinction from Trinity Theological Seminary. Mitch and his wife, Susan, live in Auburn and have four daughters. You can visit his website at www.mitchkruse.com.

D.J. Williams has been in the entertainment industry for twenty years. His writing credits include *Restoration Road* with Mitch Kruse, *The Disillusioned*, *Waking Lazarus*, and contributing writer for *Holy Bible*: *Mosaic*. Based in Los Angeles, D.J. continues to develop, produce, direct, and write for television, film, and print.

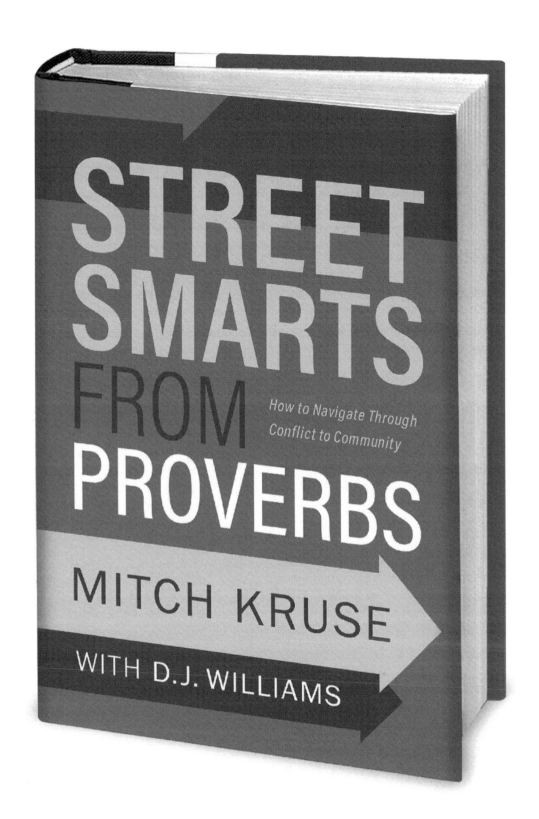

GET YOUR COPY TODAY!

WWW.MITCHKRUSE.COM

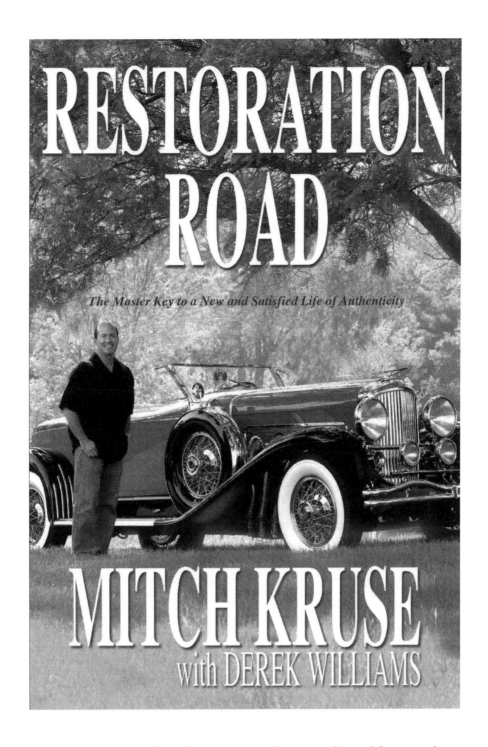

Discover your restoration journey through a 12-week experience

(Book, DVD, and Study Guide ideal for individuals or groups)

WWW.MITCHKRUSE.COM

THE RESTORATION ROAD WITH MITCH KRUSE

Teaching the Bible through stories of restoration

in order to connect culture with Christ.

AIRS ON MORE THAN 60 TELEVISION CHANNELS WORLDWIDE.
EPISODES ARE ALSO AVAILABLE ON DEMAND.

WWW.MITCHKRUSE.COM

Made in United States
Orlando, FL
13 January 2022

13383887R00059